L I F E
in the
Old Dogs
Y E T

A short amble in Ireland

by

Richard Guise

with contributions from
David Hayes, Andy McDonald and Peter Toon

Life In The Old Dogs Yet

Foreword

One of the real challenges facing not just individuals but Britain as a whole is a re-evaluation the role and lifestyle expected of the retired. And – let's not forget – this is actually a 'good news' story: people are living longer and often more healthily than ever before. And as the 'baby-boomers' swell their ranks even more, I'm delighted to draw attention to this particular group of the recently retired among my constituents. To these four men, the sixties are clearly an age not of challenges but of opportunities: in this case an opportunity to break new ground, stretch their legs, breathe the fresh air of the Atlantic coast and meet new people happy to share their own views on life. May we all be inspired by their outlook and entertained by this tale of their short adventure.

Nicky Morgan MP

Life In The Old Dogs Yet

Pre-Amble

One Friday Night, Summer 2015

Several counties could claim to be at 'the heart of rural England', but the one that grabbed this phrase for its slogan is Leicestershire. At the heart of rural Leicestershire lies the village of Quorn. At the heart of Quorn stands the Royal Oak and at the heart of the Royal Oak, one lazy Friday evening in summer, stood a short man in spectacles named Hayes (the man, not the specs.)

Hayes was a professional fixer. And a mastermind. Having masterminded the transformation of the local council's cranky recycling operation into a well-oiled machine, he quit while he was ahead, marching off in his smart suit to retirement. Tidy bins, however, mean tidy votes and a prompt step sideways from council to councillor soon meant Mr Hayes had now become Councillor Hayes.

That Friday night, though, as on most Friday nights, Councillor Hayes was merely Drinker Hayes. Prodding the man leaning next to him at the bar, he enquired, in an accent less from the heart of rural England than from 'Saaff' London:

"Hey, Guisey, you ever read 'Round Ireland With a Fridge'?"

Though the subject was out of the blue, the target was not. Another short man, minus spectacles but plus greying beard, Guise regarded himself as a travel writer. Unfortunately no publisher had regarded him as such for several years, but Guise was keen for the label – with its hint of the exotic – to stick. His own accent bore the exotic dullness of Derbyshire.

"The Tony Hawks book? I think I started it. Why?"

"We should do that."

"What? Walk round Ireland with a fridge?"

"Yeah. Well, with something else."

"Like what?"

"I'll leave the details to you."

"What about a grudge?"

"Round Ireland with a grudge? Sounds a bit dangerous. Anyway, I'll leave the details to you."

This phrase, no doubt usually addressed to an office of subordinates, had clearly stood him in good stead during his long career. Hayes was a concept man.

Another Friday Night, Summer 2015

For a few weeks, Guise proceeded to forget all about Ireland, until another Friday night, this time a few yards down the road at the White Hart. Had it been Saturday, it would have been the Blacksmith's Arms. With seven pubs to choose from, revellers regularly spill onto the village streets, as taxis drop off more and more punters, dressed in less and less as the evening progresses. Someone compared Quorn in summer to Malaga on a Saturday night. On this evening, though, the clientele at the White Hart was of a certain age and fully dressed. They included Hayes and Guise.

"Hey, Guisey, you got our trip planned yet?"

"What trip?"

"Walking round Ireland, you know?"

"What, just you and me?"

"He might want to come too."

Hayes was nodding at the man behind Guise, another chap of short stature, minus spectacles, minus beard, but plus a shiny pate that belied his youthful looks.

"Hey, Toon," said Guise. "D'you want to walk round Ireland with him and me?"

"Yeah, all right. Whereabouts?"

"West coast," said Hayes.

"Yeah, all right," said Toon. "Another pint?"

Toon's accent was from rugged Coalville, the jewel of North-West Leicestershire, where the boy had begun his meteoric rise from coal to shale gas, office junior to senior surveyor and the back streets of a pit town to the posh side of Quorn. But nowadays his theodolite was closely focused on a not-too-distant horizon, where hovered the tempting prospect of retirement.

Another pint or two drowned the subject for the rest of the evening, but this time Guise awoke the next day still harbouring a vague memory of some Celtic concept or other. The email he despatched enquired of Hayes and Toon whether they were serious. 'Deadly', replied Hayes. 'Let's walk the west coast, starting at Dublin.' Geography, it turns out, is not Hayes' strong suit. 'The west coast of Ireland is about 1600 miles long,' replied Guise. 'Anywhere in particular?' Hayes' response was predictable: 'I'll leave the details to you.'

Toon, meanwhile, held his fire. He was still busy persuading the north-west of England that 'shale gas extraction' was a nicer term than 'fracking'.

October 2015

As it happened, Guise was about to visit an old friend in the Emerald Isle, one who'd made absent appearances (a tricky concept) in several of his travelogues under the moniker 'the Wanderer'. Though the Wanderer had for many years lived under the sunny skies of southern France, for reasons known only to himself he'd recently purchased a second home under the cloudy skies of Ireland's salad cream capital, County Mayo. On return to Quorn (England's artificial beef capital), Guise emptied his copious Ryanair pockets of their leaflets on Mayo, Galway and Connemara. While including the Wanderer himself in any plans was out of the question (since the

Wanderer doesn't do plans), the region around his friend's new home had seemed ideal for coastal walks.

A draft plan followed, just to see if he'd picked up the right idea. It comprised a five-day tour of Connemara, from Galway to Westport, partly by scheduled bus and partly on foot. The longest walking day would be about 18 miles. After double-checking the bus timetables and identifying suitable B&Bs, Guise copied the schedule into an email and clicked on Send.

In pretty short order a message bounced back from Councillor Hayes: '18 miles?! Surely the pubs in Ireland aren't that far apart.'

Toon held his fire.

Guise called a meeting.

One Saturday Night, January 2016

Onto the White Hart's map table Guise emptied his miscellaneous leaflets and maps of County Mayo. ('Map table' may not be its official designation.)

"That's great," said Hayes. "This is my friend Dermot. He thinks we should go to County Kerry."

Despite his name, Dermot had an English accent and proceeded to beguile the three of them with the wonders of Kerry's Dingle Peninsula. It certainly seemed to fit the bill and had one attraction that even Connemara couldn't offer: a resident dolphin called Fungie. Not only did Connemara have no resident dolphin called Fungie; it had no resident dolphin at all. So beguiling was beguiler Dermot that another White Hart regular was drawn to the map table.

"Ayup," said McDonald, "what's going on here?"

The unspoken words 'without me involved' were left hanging in the air. A tall – and, more recently, slightly wide – man, McDonald had neither spectacles nor beard nor shiny pate. What he did possess was so many bucketfuls of charisma that from the back of his Fiat he sells small tubs of charisma, topped with kudos and with a side order of street cred. Since retirement from the council's housing department, McDonald had become something of a property typhoon. (Spellcheck, please don't change that word. And, by the way, change your own name to Spelling Checker – I'm not a witch.) Like an oriental hurricane, he'd blown through the local housing market until he owned more houses than you could shake a scaffolding pole at.

"We're fleshing out a concept," said Guise. "Dermot here thinks we should go to Dingle."

"Doesn't he like you then? Ha ha."

McDonald should have been on the stage. It left at five o'clock. Ha ha.

When not impersonating Tommy Trinder or Ted Ray, he speaks with an accent even more local than Toon's – which, as McDonald was born just two miles up the road in Loughborough, is not surprising.

"Count me in!" he said.

The three shorties counted McDonald in.

Dingle is a hilly peninsula in the south-west of Ireland. The four amigos having more or less agreed on it, Hayes offered Guise an extra map. It covered the *north*-west of Ireland.

"Yeah, thanks," said Guise, popping it into his expanding yellow bag.

"Oh, and here are some leaflets I found," added Hayes. They focused on Londonderry, about 300 miles from Dingle and in another country.

"Yeah, right," grunted Guise, as he swung the yellow bag over his shoulder, nearly knocking Toon over in the process. "I'll be in touch."

Another Saturday Night, January 2016

For the second time in a month Hayes, Guise, Toon and McDonald gathered around the White Hart's map table, diaries to hand. Three of the diaries were traditional paper-based affairs; one was a smartphone. The odd one out belonged to Toon who, though he had by now finally retired, still retained the trinkets of workdom to ensure he was at all times organised and at the ready. He'd forgotten his reading glasses.

"What about the week of March 14th?" asked Guise, in the chair.

"Council meeting," said Hayes.

"OK. What about April 11th?"

"Fine," said Hayes.

"Fine," said McDonald.

"I can't read this screen," said Toon.

"Try these glasses," said Hayes.

"'S'alright," said Toon. "I can use these." Out of his jacket pocket, the erstwhile surveyor pulled a small pair of binoculars and, to the sound of rising eyebrows (a very subtle sound, admittedly), proceeded to examine his smartphone from a distance.

"Can you hold it against that wall, mate?" he asked.

Sighing a sigh of disbelief, McDonald dutifully held the phone a table's length away from Toon. It should be noted that Toon is often what used to be described as 'adjacent', which is to say that, while he seems to be physically present, he's actually in a parallel universe. It's called ToonWorld.

"Is April early this year?" he asked.

"Give it 'ere," said Hayes. "Yes, Toony, you're free the week beginning April 11th."

"Out on April 11th then," said Guise, "back on April 16th." He snapped closed his own diary and sat back in his chair. "Any more business?"

McDonald looked at him askance. "Yes," he said. "Where are we going? What are we going to do? Will there be breakfasts? How many pants should I take?" He paused and leaned forward on the map table. "Who's sleeping with who?"

"With whom," said Guise, who appears in this book courtesy of the Worshipful Society of Pedants.

"Exactly."

"Don't worry, mate. I'll be in touch." McDonald pushed a plastic bag towards him. "What's that?" asked Guise

"Thought you might like some leaflets," said McDonald.

February 2016

Most of the next month was spent dealing with the controversial subject of Roger.

Roger is a close friend of Hayes, with whom the latter had evidently spent some intimate moments and whom he seemed keen to bring on the Irish adventure. To float the idea, Hayes took Roger to the posh side of Quorn to visit the Toons. Roger, reported Toon later, was about three feet tall with a pungent odour, prompting his immediate consignment to the Toonian garage.

Though short, three feet was at least one foot too tall for Ryanair's cabin luggage and so, reluctantly, Hayes was forced to accept that Roger the Rucksack would not be accompanying him. For a week or two he floated the idea of Carol the Camel, even distributing to the others a disturbing photograph of himself mounted on Carol, but eventually Carol too was to find herself inconsistent with Ryanair's regulations ('Dromedaries, Camels and other Ungulates' subsection).

One Thursday morning, March 2016

The date of the final planning meeting finally arrived. Flights had been booked, bed and breakfasts reserved. A series of emails distributed by McDonald had already made it clear he believed several vital decisions had yet to be taken. He'd discovered, for example, that on the afternoon of Day 3, a half-hour period seemed somehow to have escaped any pre-planned activities at all.

According to Guise, however, the only vital pieces missing from the jigsaw were the data for online check-in and the money he was owed. Accordingly he'd already asked his fellow adventurers to bring cash and passports.

The rendezvous was to be at Guise's abode at 10.30 am. After querying the time, Hayes had eventually accepted that there might be two 10.30s in one 24-hour period. At the appointed hour, Guise heard a rumbling outside. A glance through the window revealed McDonald struggling up the drive with a huge suitcase on wheels.

"Is check-in this way?" he asked.

Speechless for once, Guise waved him through to the lounge, where Toon was already pouring over a new map table and puzzling why two of the maps thereon were of the Swiss Alps and Lake Constance.

"What's that, you idiot?" asked Toon.

"Well, that's nice, isn't it?" said McDonald. "I've dragged this halfway across the village for your benefit, mate."

With that, he unzipped the case to reveal about a dozen knapsacks of various sizes, ages and hues, which he proceeded to empty onto the carpet.

"It's to show you what size bag you can take."

"We know what size bag we can take. Guisey's already sent us the measurements."

At this point, Hayes turned up, noticeably short of breath.

"They've closed the path. I've walked all round the village," he panted. "What's... what's all this?"

Ignoring all comments, Typhoon McDonald proceeded to open one of the smaller knapsacks and empty onto the table about thirty maps.

"I've already got the local maps," said Guise.

"You haven't got these," said McDonald. "They're of Devon and Cornwall."

"And Lincolnshire," added Toon, who'd started to go through them. "I like maps, McDonald, but we're going to Ireland."

"I think we should start a map database," explained McDonald. It was clear this wasn't what the others regarded as an explanation.

"Very nice," said Hayes. "Have a doughnut."

Guise, who was beginning to wonder if he'd eaten too much Cheddar and was having one of those irrational cheese dreams, spoke slowly: "Can we get down to business? Money and passports?" Hearing his own voice, he concluded this wasn't a dream after all.

McDonald had already paid up, but had forgotten his passport. Hayes had remembered his passport, but forgotten the cash. Toon had remembered the cash but forgotten his passport. Well, fifty per cent used to be a pass mark.

Following a brief lecture by McDonald entitled 'The Pros and Cons of Gore-Tex Luggage in Twenty-First-Century Europe', the meeting broke up in something approaching disarray.

And people say that, of the two largest British Isles, the more disorganised is Ireland.

Toon searches for a gap in his diary.

Guise practises for his drinking badge.

Hayes (right) wonders where Ireland is.

McDonald enters the second hour of his lecture on luggage.

A small selection from the planning materials consulted.

Risings

One Monday, April 2016. Quorn to Killarney.

In Quorn, the day dawned dry and dull. Not that Hayes, Guise, Toon or McDonald would know that, since by dawn they were already at East Midlands Airport. Best start this chapter again...

In Quorn, the pre-dawn was dark. Very dark. For some time the village had been one of the pilot areas for 'Part-Night Lighting', a project aimed at reducing costs by switching off most street lights between midnight and 5.30am. Despite objections from the odd nervous burglar and sun-worshipping badger that it had become harder to break into the village's houses and gardens respectively, the switch-off had been hailed a success. A rare example of councils doing something right. Much of the cost saving, however, had been lost by paying for a sturdy notice on every single 'part-night' lamppost explaining to Mr Witterer of Chunter Cottage, Moaning Street, Quorn, that the light was not faulty, merely off.

The rendezvous having been agreed as Guise's house at 5am, it was dark. Very dark. (Oh, for goodness sake, get on with it!) All right... as Guise stood outside his home, he saw a small, wavering light to his left, like a one-eyed cat with a limp. Toon. To his right there emerged from Tom Long's Swamp a pair of wavering lights, like a cat with loose eye balls.

Hayes and McDonald. Out of the right-hand gloom emerged McDonald, with a back-pack precisely measured to Ryanair's requirements, and Hayes with a slightly more modest backpack. Out of the left-hand gloom emerged a huge, pre-deployment parachute, complete with spare 'chute, pull cords, emergency light and whistle. Inside the package was Toon.

"Morning, chaps," said Toon.

"What on earth's that?" asked Guise.

"Shh," said McDonald.

"Where's my dog?" asked Hayes, raising for the benefit of the torch beams a piece of string, notable for the absence of anything canine on its end.

"Shh," said McDonald.

Into view rolled the taxi. Into the taxi rolled three of the boys, followed by a clambering, clattering Toon. Off to the airport rolled the whole kit and caboodle.

*

In early December 1999, keen to have an excuse ready to avoid any millennium party, Guise had registered as a licensed taxi driver and signed up for night shifts with a local private hire company. New Year's Eve came and went without any of the inflated fares he'd been hoping for – but with the memory of an unforgettable request from a fare picked up from a suburban party at ten minutes to midnight...

"Where to, sir?"

"Anywhere but here, mate."

Though Guise gave up the night job shortly afterwards (mission having been accomplished), every taxi driver picking him up since had had to deal with the same tedious questions endured this early morning sixteen years later by the quiet Asian driver:

"I used to drive a taxi, you know?"

"Really, sir?"

"Night shift. This the end of your shift?"

"Yes, sir."

"Same shift every day?"

"Yep."

"Much business?"

"Normal. Oh, except the four scantily clad girls who waved me down in Loughborough and made me pull over in a quiet lay-by while they stripped naked and changed seats, brushing their nubile young bodies against my face, before I dropped them off in Sileby."

Actually, he just said: "Normal. Steady."

As they all did.

Ironically, the only millennium party invitation Guise had received – and been relieved to turn down -- was from the woman he'd subsequently move in with and who'd just waved the four of them off in pre-dawn Quorn from the house where the party had taken place. While Toon and McDonald had also whispered their goodbyes to their beloveds in the previous hour, Councillor Hayes was aiming to keep an eagle eye open in the Emerald Isle for any eligible lady who might fall for his suave and sophisticated charms.

"Irish farmers' gels, y'know. Dairy maids. They know how to handle a man. Know what I mean?"

The others suspected they did.

*

On arrival at the airport, boarding passes were duly distributed and the long queue for security joined. Having pulled out their carefully stowed passports and transparent bags of liquids, Hayes, Guise and McDonald – and most of the queue – were entertained by Toon, as he first disentangled himself from his packs, rummaged around in the smaller, then the larger, for the passport, which he proceeded to secure in his teeth while repeating the search, this time for his transparent bag. This in turn having finally been discovered, it had to be deposited on the floor while its owner, face now red and perspiring, wrestled himself out of the top few layers of clothing (not an easy task with a passport in your teeth) before collecting from the floor his various unappended appendages and swaying unsteadily off, straps all a-dangle, and thus allowing the patient passengers behind to rejoin the queue from which Toon's gymnastics had temporarily detached them.

As he approached the other three, Typhoon McDonald was in full swing.

"Hey, look at this." He was reading the newspaper. "If you fly from Dublin to New York you can do your U.S. immigration at Dublin. How great is that? Avoid all those queues and the miserable American officials. And why do you think that is?" The question was rhetorical: when McDonald's on a roll, he supplies both questions and answers, free of charge. "It's the Irish influence, ain't it? America's full of 'em. New York especially. St Patrick's Day and all that. Special privileges for the Irish. Here's Toon. Hey, Toony! Now you've found all your extraneous bits and pieces, have you got your spare tissues at the ready?" At this, the Typhoon pulled from his pocket what looked suspiciously like a small toilet roll without the middle bit. Suspicions were immediately confirmed. "Never know when you'll be taken short, do you? Got yours, Toon?"

"No."

"Councillor?"

"No."

"Guisey?"

Captain Careful[1] withdrew a wad of tissues from his own pocket. "Yes, sir."

Apart from the delay while Guise – possibly the western world's least likely terrorist – was extracted from the queue, taken aside and frisked, the remainder of the journey passed without incident. Unless you count gathering storm clouds.

*

By the the time Dublin's airport bus deposited the foursome on O'Connell Street, it was still not long after nine and drizzling steadily. Slate-grey skies seemed to cover the city streets with a thin layer of metallic dullness. Hunched pedestrians trudged past, shoulders raised as psychological protection against another miserable Monday morning. It looked less like the Emerald Isle in April than Franz Josef Land in bleak midwinter.

The boys' spirits, though, were high. After months of planning they'd finally arrived and nothing was going to interfere with the chance to spend an hour or so in a new city, before heading off for the train to the west. They even deputed Captain Careful to negotiate with the bus driver before he sped off.

---

1   For source of monikers, see later.

"Can we use these tickets to resume the journey to the station on the next bus?"

"No."

"We have to buy new tickets?"

"Yes."

"Even though we've only stopped so the old fella can go to the toilet?" He indicated the Councillor, if only because the latter had for some reason assumed a distinctly unnatural stance.

"Well, theoretically that makes no difference." He was wavering. "But..."

"Yes?"

"Sure, give me one of your tickets."

Guise handed over his own for the driver to scribble something on the back.

"Show that to the next driver," he advised. "They all know me."

And with that he drove off. The four gathered round to examine Guise's ticket. 'Good for four passengers', it read, followed by the driver's signature.

"A free passport to Dublin!" hailed McDonald.

"We'll see," said Captain Careful.

*

Ninety-nine years, eleven months and seventeen days before, something significant happened hereabouts. On the morning of 24th April 1916, Easter Monday, the central area of Dublin where the boys had alighted (and at that time part of the United Kingdom) was seized by about a thousand members of the Irish Volunteers and Irish Citizen Army. Police were taken prisoner, civilians evacuated and barricades erected. About 400 of the militia marched from Liberty Hall to the General Post Office, where they hoisted Republican flags and listened to their leader, a teacher named Patrick Pearse, read out a carefully prepared proclamation of an Irish Republic. An act of rebellion against the British government, at that time rather preoccupied with other enemies across the Channel. The Easter Rising was not as well-armed as the leaders had hoped, since at virtually the last minute weaponry sent from Germany had been intercepted by British forces and, after six days and 500 deaths, was finally extinguished and its leaders executed. The Irish Free State, however, was to be finally established six years later.

Like any dutiful nation, the Irish had gone to town in marking the centenary of events leading up to their birth as a state. O'Connell Street, that grey Monday morning, was everywhere speckled with the date '1916', like numerate confetti. The boys were not unaware of this centenary – Typhoon McDonald had made sure of that. After guiding them to his eponymous fast-food outlet for a late breakfast ('late' being seven hours after their own April rising), he whisked them into the building central to the Rising, and still dominating O'Connell Street: the General Post Office.

And a grand, traditional post office it was too: high ceilings, marble columns, polished metal grilles, elegant writing desks. The lot. Pride of place fell to a bronze statue of Cúchulainn, a mythological Irish hero who, mortally injured in battle, still managed to tie himself upright to a pillar so that, even in death, he could face his enemies. The statue had been created in the 1930s as a memorial to the Rising and beneath it are inscribed the names of the signatories of the proclamation, declared outside this very building on that Easter Monday a hundred years ago. Again, classic patriotic marketing: forge a mental link between modern leaders and previous national heroes, real or not. Incidentally, the oft-repeated phrase that Pearse proclaimed the Republic 'from the steps of' the General Post Office seems questionable, since there are no steps outside this building. However, it's said that Pearse, a short man, raised himself up on a pedestal at the base of one of the columns.

Replicas of the declaration appeared wherever the boys went in Dublin – indeed wherever they went that week in Ireland: in shop windows, on pub walls, by reception desks. So it's worth looking at what it actually said.

Poblacht na hÉireann
THE PROVISIONAL GOVERNMENT OF THE IRISH REPUBLIC TO
THE PEOPLE OF IRELAND
IRISHMEN AND IRISHWOMEN:
In the name of God and of the dead generations from which she receives her old tradition of nationhood, Ireland, through us, summons her children to her flag and strikes for her freedom.

Having organised and trained her manhood through her secret revolutionary organisation, the Irish Republican Brotherhood, and through her open military organisations, the Irish Volunteers and the Irish Citizen Army, having patiently perfected her discipline, having resolutely waited for the right moment to reveal itself, she now seizes that moment, and supported by her exiled children in America and by gallant allies in Europe, but relying in the first on her own strength, she strikes in full confidence of victory.

We declare the right of the people of Ireland to the ownership of Ireland and to the unfettered control of Irish destinies, to be sovereign and indefeasible. The long usurpation of that right by a foreign people and government has not extinguished the right, nor can it ever be extinguished except by the destruction of the Irish people. In every generation the Irish people have asserted their right to national freedom and sovereignty; six times during the past three hundred years they have asserted it in arms. Standing on that fundamental right and again asserting it in arms in the face of the world, we hereby proclaim the Irish Republic as a Sovereign Independent State, and we pledge our lives and the lives of our comrades in arms to the cause of its freedom, of its welfare, and of its exaltation among the nations.

The Irish Republic is entitled to, and hereby claims, the allegiance of every Irishman and Irishwoman. The Republic guarantees religious and civil liberty, equal rights and equal opportunities to all its citizens, and declares its resolve to pursue the happiness and prosperity of the whole nation and of all its parts, cherishing all of the children of the nation equally, and oblivious of the differences carefully fostered by an alien Government, which have divided a minority from the majority in the past.

Until our arms have brought the opportune moment for the establishment of a permanent National Government, representative of the whole people of Ireland and elected by the suffrages of all her men and women, the Provisional Government, hereby constituted, will administer the civil and military affairs of the Republic in trust for the people.

We place the cause of the Irish Republic under the protection of the Most High God, Whose blessing we invoke upon our arms, and we pray that no one who serves that cause will dishonour it by cowardice, inhumanity, or rapine. In this supreme hour the Irish nation must, by its valour and discipline, and by the readiness of its children to sacrifice themselves for the common good, prove itself worthy of the august destiny to which it is called.

Signed on behalf of the Provisional Government:

THOMAS J. CLARKE, SEAN MacDIARMADA, THOMAS MacDONAGH, P. H. PEARSE, EAMONN CEANNT, JAMES CONNOLLY, JOSEPH PLUNKETT

A classic. God, ancestry, comradeship, honour, valour, sacrifice, militarism, egalitarianism, sovereignty, independence, freedom... all boxes ticked. Throw in a common enemy ('an alien Government', i.e. Britain) and a name-check for a rich benefactor (America) and you've got an excellent model from which to construct your own declaration of independence, should you find yourself in charge of your own beleaguered nation one Monday morning.

*

Sated with history, the boys found themselves back at the O'Connell Street bus stop to continue their journey. Queueing diligently at the bus stop marked Airlink 747, they watched the Airlink 747 bus pull in about fifty metres away, unload its passengers, pull out into the traffic again and sail by, completely ignoring them.

A nearby tourist guide saw their dismay. She was about twenty years old and dressed entirely in green.

"Ah yes, you'll be wanting the Airlink bus to the station?"

"Yes," said Hayes, as always strategically positioned next to the nearest female.

"Well, they do sometimes stop up there."

"But there's no bus stop there."

"That's true enough."

As Airlink buses arrived every fifteen minutes, the boys started to move towards the spot without the stop.

"But they sometimes stop here," the girl called after them.

They froze and looked back.

"How do you know which?" asked McDonald.

"Well, it depends on the driver. Some stop up there, some stop here."

The boys looked at each other and back at the girl.

"Look," she said. "You go up there and I'll wait down here. If the next one stops here, I'll hold it till you get here."

And sure enough, the next bus did indeed pass the boys by and pull in by the green girl. After lugging their kit back down the road again and thanking their emerald saviour, they pushed a panting Guise in first to show the driver the note on his ticket.

"Ah yes," he said. "I know him. You boys are all right with me. Hop aboard now. Don't hang around."

*

Many years ago, the Wanderer (Guise's Westport friend) had been contracted to undertake a survey of bus users in Dublin. At a suburban bus stop, he was going through the questionnaire with one elderly lady.

"How would you rate the bus service in Dublin?" he read. "Good, average or poor?"

"Poor," she stated without hesitation.

"And why do you think the service is poor?"

After thinking long and hard, she delivered her verdict: "Badness."

*

The boys' own friendly driver duly deposited them at Heuston Station, though not before undertaking an unexpected handbrake turn that deposited Hayes and Toon firmly onto the floor. Brushing themselves down, the boys marched with varying pace towards the station's facilities, pace being determined by bladder capacity. While the overriding sensation for (almost) everyone on leaving a public convenience is relief, this is clearly not enough for the Irish. True to a national character that demands a more personal revelation, the railway company has installed a small machine at the toilet exit inviting the user to press one of four buttons to express their sense of satisfaction. Below the row of buttons are the words 'Happy or Not?'. A deep green smiley face presumably indicates 'Completely relieved, thank you'; a lighter green, rather quizzical face for 'OK for a while anyway'; a pink, somewhat strained face for 'That was harder than I expected'; and the red face of despair for 'No paper!'.

All four boys having emerged either completely or partially relieved and McDonald having been firmly escorted past the temptations of the Galway

Hooker (a pub not a person), they presented themselves at the station's ticket counter, Guise first.

"We're going to Killarney, but coming back from Tralee."

"You'll be wanting a return to Tralee."

"If you say so."

"Don't forget to get off at Killarney."

"No."

"Ask 'er if we can get a group ticket," interjected Hayes.

"Can we..."

"No." She could hear through the glass.

"Ask 'er if I can get a pensioner's discount."

"You ask her..."

"No," she said.

"Ask 'er..."

"No," said Guise. Whatever it was. Probably a date.

After counting out a king's ransom in euros, Guise retreated to let the others ransom their own monarchs. The kitty was to be reserved for food and drink. Well, drink mostly. Let's be honest: for Guinness.

Once more hauling McDonald back from the clutches of the Hooker (10.30am was a little early to start, even for him), the boys scrambled aboard the swish-looking, yellow-green-and-white carriages of the 11 o'clock service to Cork (change at Mallow for Tralee). With plenty of space available, they spread themselves over eight seats and two tables and raised a small cheer as the train pulled out of the station to set them off on their Irish adventure. As Guise handed round a ragged 'lucky dip' bag of sweets and Hayes gave a brief 'whooo-uup!' on his swanee whistle, one or two Irish eyes cast a nervous glance in their direction. Was this a pensioners' outing, a day release from the asylum or an ageing schoolboys' field trip? Or a meticulously planned sortie by four retired professionals? Take your pick.

*

Iarnród Éireann, the jaunty-sounding operator of almost all of Ireland's railways, has about 2,700 route kilometres to manage. Just as Britain's network radiates from London, Ireland's radiates from Dublin, mostly from

Heuston, a terminus originally named Kingsbridge but renamed in the sixties after Seán Heuston, one of the executed leaders of the Easter Rising and who'd worked on the railways. As I'm sure you know, Ireland's mainlines are broad gauge, like Spain's but unlike Britain's, and of the eight main long-distance routes in the Republic, the south-westernmost reaches Cork in the south and Tralee in the west. You'll be beside yourselves to learn that it's operated by 201-class diesel locomotives and overcome with the news that the one hauling the boys along that Monday morning was none other than Locomotive 232. Oh, yes.

Among Iron Rod's modern conveniences is wi-fi and when the attraction of Dublin's industrial suburbs began to fade (after about a minute), three of the boys turned on and logged in. Hayes played idly with his swanee.

"Hey," said McDonald, snatching Toon's mobile, "Toony's got an iPhone! Bet that cost you a few bob."

"Not that much," retorted Toon. "Give it 'ere."

"Bit of a small screen, mate. You want one o' these." He flashed his own phone for the carriage's occupants to admire. "Windows phone. Guess how much it cost me." No one did. "Nowt. Nothin'. Zip nada, as they say in California. And look how big the screen is! £8.50 a month and a free phone. Hours of calls, zillions of texts, waggabytes of data. £8.50 a month! Can't say no, can you? You don't want one o' them iPhones, you want one o' these."

The oddity of McDonald's salesmanship, which is indeed hard to resist, is that he never has anything to sell. All the effort goes into selling someone else's product. Vicariovendism. That's what you want. Not your autism or your narcissism. Vicariovendism. That's what you need.

"Look," he exclaimed triumphantly. "Guisey's got a Windows phone too!"

Guise was paying no attention. As soon as Iron Rod's wi-fi had clicked in, a cacophony of bleeps and warbles had emanated from his own phone and he was now endeavouring to kill them off one by one.

"Emails, texts, voicemails, missed calls..." he mumbled to himself. "How can all these people want me? I've only been away a few hours." Munching the Marmite sandwiches he'd brought from home, he tapped and frowned at the screen. "The world was a better place before mobiles."

"I just leave mine switched off," commented Hayes, still fingering his swanee. "Look, 'ere's the gel with the coffee."

With Hayes trying his luck with a woman forty years his junior, McDonald now reading the paper and Toon just sitting happily in ToonWorld, Guise listened to a voicemail, sighed and walked up the train in search of any bright-looking Irish person for advice on leading zeroes in Irish phone numbers. Months after he'd reserved that night's rooms at Murphy's Bar in Killarney, they'd left it to the very day of arrival before asking if he still wanted them. Following a well-spoken man's advice, he pressed the numbers. Unobtainable. Again. Unobtainable. Drop the zero. Invalid number. Add another zero. Invalid number. Try original again. Ring ring. Eyebrows by now almost on the ceiling, he managed to convince a lady with the voice of a child chewing rope that the four of them were genuinely in her country and would genuinely arrive as scheduled.

So few people are interested in the books Guise writes that he hadn't sold a single printed version through Amazon for two years. Until today, an email told him. Just as he'd left the country, two books had been sold. Two! Several complicated calls later, he'd managed to get them out of his stock remotely and on the way to the post office... at a cost probably in excess of any profit. By the time he'd sorted out this and several other urgent matters, he switched off his phone with a flourish.

"Any sign of the tea trolley, chaps?"

"Gone, mate. You should pay more attention."

*

With the train journey scheduled to take about three hours, Guise handed round a printed questionnaire. Not to the other passengers, it should be stressed – although 'How long can you stand the inane prattling by these English blokes?' would have been a valid enough question. His unending mission in life is to sort order from chaos and this, a single sheet of A4 that would take at most ten minutes to complete, was to be the chance for each of the four to contribute equally to their own characterisation in these pages, an opportunity they all acknowledged to be an excellent idea. However, the ultimate fate of these questionnaires is ample evidence of how futile this mission is. Instead of completing them in the idle hours between Dublin and Mallow, each of his three friends simply filed the document. Eleven days later, i.e. *after* returning to England, McDonald admitted he'd misplaced his and asked Guise to forward him an electronic version. A further week after this, Toon discovered his own half-completed copy had gone missing and begged a new printed version, his own printer having gone the way of most computer equipment he touches, which is to say kaput. Hayes' contribution finally surfaced a full five weeks after the end of the trip.

What follows are the completed forms, verbatim.

Self-Assessment Personality Profile: A McDonald

The name my parents called me when I was a child was:
Get out now.
The name I'd prefer to be called on tour is:
Your Highness.
My knowledge of Ireland before the tour could be written on:
Paper or parchment.
The most likely reason I'll have to visit the nurse on tour is:
Because she's good-looking.
Information useful to the nurse if I am delivered to her
unconscious:
My wallet's empty.
The only guilty secret I'm prepared to reveal is:
That my arse cream works.
The one luxury I'd like to take to the desert island is:
A complete Aldi supermarket and delivery lorry.
The person I'd most like to share that luxury is:
The wife ('cos then she'd be there with me).
When they make a film of this book, the actor most suitable
for playing me would be:
Alfie Bass or Arthur Mullard.
If I were to sum up my appearance in one word, it would be:
Staggering.
If I were to sum up my personality in one word, it would be:
Gamine.

Self-Assessment Personality Profile: P Toon

The name my parents called me when I was a child was:
Ah (Our) Peter.
The name I'd prefer to be called on tour is:
Anything but 'Ah Peter'.
My knowledge of Ireland before the tour could be written on:
My little toenail.
The most likely reason I'll have to visit the nurse on tour is:
Earache. (Nothing to do with McDonald!)
Information useful to the nurse if I am delivered to her
unconscious:
Do not resuscitate (if admitted with earache).
The only guilty secret I'm prepared to reveal is:
**Stealing a packet of crumpets that turned out to be
mouldy when I got them home.**
The one luxury I'd like to take to the desert island is:
A pillow.
The person I'd most like to share that luxury is:
... probably not going to accept an invitation.
When they make a film of this book, the actor most suitable
for playing me would be:
Dennis Waterman.
If I were to sum up my appearance in one word, it would be:
Handsome.
If I were to sum up my personality in one word, it would be:
Confused.

Self-Assessment Personality Profile: R Guise

The name my parents called me when I was a child was:

The lad. (They were nothing if not observant.)

The name I'd prefer to be called on tour is:

Captain Careful.

My knowledge of Ireland before the tour could be written on:

Twiggy's bosom.

The most likely reason I'll have to visit the nurse on tour is:

Advanced insanity from spending a week with this lot.

Information useful to the nurse if I am delivered to her unconscious:

He breathes so lightly that a second opinion should be sought before delivery to the knacker's yard.

The only guilty secret I'm prepared to reveal is:

I put some dosh on the Foxsh***ers to win the Premier League.

The one luxury I'd like to take to the desert island is:

A solar-powered fridge packed with bottles of Rioja.

The person I'd most like to share that luxury is:

Fiona Bruce.

When they make a film of this book, the actor most suitable for playing me would be:

Short and round.

If I were to sum up my appearance in one word, it would be:

Shortandround.

If I were to sum up my personality in one word, it would be:

Long-suffering.

Self-Assessment Personality Profile: D Hayes

The name my parents called me when I was a child was:

Who? (as they knew this name couldn't be shortened).

The name I'd prefer to be called on tour is:

Cockney Rebel

My knowledge of Ireland before the tour could be written on:

Toenail

The most likely reason I'll have to visit the nurse on tour is:

I used my Viagra tablet as a suppository.

Information useful to the nurse if I am delivered to her unconscious:

Do Not Resuscitate.

The only guilty secret I'm prepared to reveal is:

[None revealed]

The one luxury I'd like to take to the desert island is:

Toilet paper.

The person I'd most like to share that luxury is:

Lulu.

When they make a film of this book, the actor most suitable for playing me would be:

David Jason.

If I were to sum up my appearance in one word, it would be:

Stunning.

If I were to sum up my personality in one word, it would be:

Creative.

While there's a strong suggestion that some copying has been going on, the headmaster has agreed to let it go. The nurse, however, will be having a quiet talk with Hayes about the dangers of sharing lavatorial equipment with short Scottish singers.

In addition, each was asked to sum up the personality of the others in one word. These are reproduced below – and, in the interests of world peace, in a random sequence. Clearly one contributor has trouble counting words.

His Highness (A McDonald):

Manipulative

Mesmerising

Amazing

Skipper Toon[2] (P Toon):

Visionary

Other-worldly

Listens intently, but the words do not compute

Captain Careful[3] (R Guise):

Eccentric

Organised

For he's a jolly good fellow

(given that he's from Long Eaton)

The Councillor[4] (D Hayes):

Semi-intelligible

Talks rubbish intelligently

Enthusiastic

---

2 Allocated in the absence of any specific suggestion of his own, Toon being a qualified yachtmaster.

3 Two captains are better than one. (Or are they?)

4 See footnote on next page.

*5

The journey sped past and pretty soon Loco 232 had whisked them across the rolling green fields of Leinster all the way to County Tipperary. As they pulled in at Thurles station, His Highness recalled a visit he'd made here in the 1970s, with his friend Barty, to deliver a trailer-load of furniture from England to a house near the town.

One evening, unsurprisingly, they found themselves in a local pub. A little more surprisingly, when the band struck up in a back room at eight o'clock on the dot, they peered through the door to see all the women sitting around the sides of the room like fourth-formers at a school dance. In trooped the men, neckerchiefs duly adjusted, to proceed at a steady pace along the lines of potential partners before enquiring of their favourite whether she'd care to... well, of course she would... and onto the dance floor they swung. At precisely nine-thirty the music stopped, to be replaced by the sound of fist crunching on chin and knee penetrating groin as a fully-fledged fight broke out among the men – and then, just as suddenly as it had started, ceased. Up struck the band and the dance resumed. Presumably with a few of the males mincing rather than gliding their way across the floor.

The next day, McDonald recalled, he and Barty enjoyed a long, lazy lunch at the house of their hosts, the furniture-buyers. Relaxing afterwards in one of the lounge's big chairs, Barty glanced toward the corner of the room and spotted something amiss, something he felt he should share with his hosts.

"You've left your immersion heater on. I can see the little light."

"What?"

---

5   When responsible for the borough's refuse collection, David Hayes was naturally referred to as 'Rubbish' Dave. When this was, with some justification, perceived as an unintended slur, an upgrade to 'Recycling' Dave was rolled out. It didn't catch on. Hayes' own subsequent request to be known as 'Upcycle' Dave is still in the in-tray. In the meantime, 'Councillor Hayes' – or simply 'The Councillor' – seems both apt and respectful. As these words had already been written by the time Hayes submitted his own suggestion of 'Cockney Rebel', he has kindly agreed to permit 'The Councillor' to be used. End of press release.

"In that little alcove. Your immersion heater's on."

His host turned.

"That little alcove is the shrine to Our Lady. The light's the perpetual light we burn for her."

Barty wondered which lady this might be, but wisely kept that question to himself.

As the train pulled out of Thurles and once more passed among the rolling green meadows of Tipperary, the mesmerising, manipulative Mr McDonald remembered that, all those years ago, he'd seen thousands of people – men, women and children – striding out across open fields. Following them, he'd come upon a huge sports stadium in the middle of farmland, many of its terraces open to the Irish skies, and discovered it to be hosting the Munster Hurling Final. Ireland's national sporting passion, hurling (or 'hoorling', as it's pronounced in these parts) is said to have been played for 3,000 years and to be the world's fastest field sport. What His Highness had come across was Semple Stadium, home of hurling in the south-west, and his assessment of it as 'huge' was spot on. With a capacity of 53,000, it's a lot bigger than Anfield or Villa Park and is the second-biggest sports stadium in all Ireland, after Dublin's Croke Park.

*

The farther west they travelled, the drier and brighter the weather, but the more dilapidated the farms. By the time they pulled into the rail junction of Mallow though, more and more evidence of recent storms was to be seen. Whole fields were under water and the slopes of surrounding hills sparkled damply in the afternoon sun. This must have been the weather that had moved east to Dublin. According to locals, the last few days had seen not only torrential rain, but hail and snow. Welcome to Ireland in April.

While the boys waited for the intently-listening but other-worldly Mr Toon to pull on the seventeen layers of clothes he'd removed when boarding, a recorded voice advised them to "mind the gap" and thanked them "for travelling neither here nor there." At least that's what it sounded like.

New train, new passengers. With less room this time, the boys squashed into two sets of double seats, opposite a large lady sitting on her own. She was to prove useful. The eccentric jolly-good fellow, Mr Guise, broached the subject McDonald had raised several weeks before and which had never been resolved.

"Who," he said with as much gravity as he could muster, "is sleeping with whom?" Large Lady focused more closely on her magazine. "We've booked one single and a room for three."

"Three beds, I hope?" asked McDonald.

"Correct. Is there anyone who actually doesn't want to be in the single?"

"I don't," said McDonald. "I want to be where the action is."

Three pairs of eyes widened. Four if you include Large Lady's.

Having written the initial of each of the other three on scraps of the Irish Times, Guise dropped them in a hat and offered it to Large Lady, who immediately got the idea. The scrap she chose bore the letter D.

"Councillor, you're in the single."

"Suits me fine."

*

While McDonald had visited this south-west corner of Ireland before, it was new territory for the others and, after de-training at Killarney's tiny, single-platform station, they all looked around eagerly as they took the short walk to the town centre through streets bathed in the late-afternoon sun. Even Toon had stuffed the outer three layers of clothes into his huge pack and finally emerged from ToonWorld (a world of barren hillsides, wind-blown campsites and raging seas).

"This is like paradise," he said. He's from Coalville, remember.

"Look at all those flags on that building," remarked Guise. "Green, white and orange. I'm not very good at flags. Is it Italy?"

"Italy's green, white and red, you buffoon." said McDonald. "Where are we?"

"Oh yeah. Ireland."

"And here's another clue: that's the town hall."

"Oh yeah. 'Course."

Check-in at Murphy's having been negotiated, the boys lugged their kit through a warren of floors and corridors to their rooms, where Hayes lurched off to his single and the rest inspected their three-bed room.

"There's only two beds," observed McDonald, sharp as a pin. "I like you chaps, but...."

"Don't worry," said Guise. "I'll go and..."

He was interrupted at the door by the enthusiastic but semi-intelligible Mr Hayes.

"I've got a spare one if any of you chaps needs it." He meant a bed.

On a sample of one, Irish hoteliers have trouble counting above zero.

Guise having sacrificed himself to the uncertainty of a night in the company of ladies' man Hayes, the boys set off in search of refreshment, led unsurprisingly by a desperate McDonald. It was nearly 4.30 after all.

*

Any normal drinker, which is to say any Englishman over fifty, needs to be advised of an important and oft-overlooked fact about Irish pubs: they don't serve beer. I'll start that again. Any normal drinker needs to be advised of an important and oft-overlooked fact about Irish pubs: they don't serve *ale*. They serve cold pop with a squirt of alcohol (lager). They serve cold engine grease with a squirt of alcohol (Murphy's stout). And they serve Guinness. Like Dyson vacuum cleaners and McDonald's 'restaurants', Guinness is a marketing triumph in which brand means everything and quality, well, less than everything. Dysons look different, but when the plastic bends they don't work. McDonald's eateries serve predictable food the world over, but unless you like spongey baps and taste-free chips, it's not actually a prediction many grown-ups want fulfilled. Likewise with Guinness. Its advertising focuses on look (seductively shiny), sound (quirkily gurgly) and environment (warmly Irish). But its taste is something like melted ball bearings. And, at least in Killarney and the rest of County Kerry, Guinness is served at Arctic temperatures. As any normal person knows, beer is not a cold drink; when properly served it's at room temperature. When properly served, in fact, it's real ale. It appears that Ireland has never heard of real ale.

So from Murphy's Bar, via O'Connell's Bar, The Laurels and back to Murphy's, it was mostly pints of Guinness that the kitty bought. One or two of them experimented with Murphy's stout and Captain Careful alternated

41

between pints and halves, but by and large it was four glasses of Arctic ball bearings at each hostelry.

As always, His Highness led the charge and engaged the bar staff. Why he hasn't hosted a TV chat show is a mystery to all who know him, since he'll broach a conversation with anyone, anywhere, and listen to anyone about anything, all the while fixing his interlocutor with his steady gaze.

"Greetings, landlord." he'd start. "Is it always sunny and warm here in Ireland?"

Or "Hello, squire. Which of these pumps will deliver a thirst-quenching drink for four weary Englishmen?"

Or "Good evening, young lady. I've got three old fellas here on day release looking for a good time in Killarney. What do you suggest?"

Actually one of his opening gambits was of some use: "Hello, mate. Any suggestions for a ten-mile walk from Killarney tomorrow?"

"Eight miles," corrected Captain Careful.

"Five, tops," suggested the Councillor.

"And five back," prompted fit, young Skipper Toon.

"Well, you lads'll decide for yourselves if you're fit or not. But there's the national park just on our doorstep here. Full o' paths and such it is. Here's a leaflet."

"That's for you, Guisey," decided McDonald.

"Has Ross Castle re-opened?" The landlord's question was directed at another customer.

"Oh, you're fine," he said. "The flood's are gone now. Here's a leaflet."

"And there's the big house." This another bar fly. "Take this leaflet."

"And the waterfall. Here's a map."

"You can take a boat across the lake."

"I'd climb the hills myself. The snow's gone now. You'll need a guidebook."

Loaded with ideas, suggestions and Guinness, the boys returned to their B&B. Loaded with yet more leaflets, last to lumber up the stairs was Guise. It was only 9.30pm, the music session in the bar hadn't even started, but eighteen hours from waking in Leicestershire to retiring in 'paradise' was more than enough for four old blokes.

Skipper Toon ready for take-off at 5am.

Iron Rod conducts a lavatorial consultation. (Photo: A. McDonald)

Loco 232 at Heuston Station, Dublin.

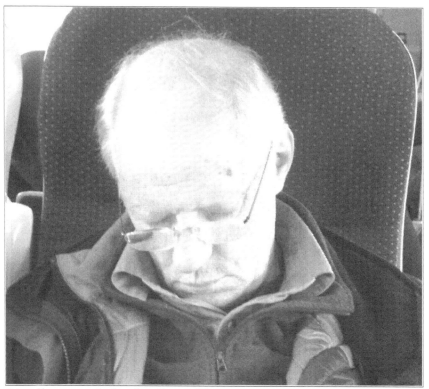

It's all too much for the Councillor.

In Murphy's Bar, Killarney.

Captain Careful's smalls under control.

Pooh Sticks in

Paradise

Tuesday, Killarney.

Early into the sharp, bright Kerry morning sprang Toon and Guise, independently, to see the lie of the land. The land beyond the bar stool, that is.

Jutting out into the North Atlantic from South-West Ireland, like the fingers of a hand reaching out to the millions of Irish men and women who've left their homeland in this direction, are five bony peninsulas. From north to south, they are the Dingle Peninsula, the Iveragh Peninsula, the Beara Peninsula, the Sheep's Head Peninsula and the Mizen Head Peninsula. Separating them are Dingle Bay, Kenmare River, Bantry Bay and Dunmanus Bay. Beyond the southernmost peninsula lies the fabulously named Roaringwater Bay. At about the spot where the knuckle of the second-northernmost finger would be, in the valley of the short River Flesk, sits the small town of Killarney. In Irish it's *Cill Airne*, meaning the church of the sloes, the sloe being the fruit of the blackthorn tree.

Though it's 25 kilometres from the sea, the town centre's only half an hour's walk from a broad stretch of fresh water called Lough Leane, beyond which rises the rugged outline of MacGillycuddy's Reeks. The odd name for this range, which includes Ireland's highest peak, comes from the clan *Mac Giolla Mochuda* and from the word *'reek'*, meaning rick or stack. *Mac Giolla Mochuda* of the *Reeks* was the clan chief and owned land hereabouts. That sunny April morning the last specks of snow still clung to sheltered corners of the mountains' north-facing slopes.

After Toon and Guise had returned, and McDonald and Hayes finally stirred themselves, the four of them assembled as scheduled for an 8.30 breakfast. No one seemed to have fallen out with anyone yet.

"Did McDonald snore?" asked Guise of Toon.

"Dunno."

"No, he wouldn't," explained McDonald. "Because he goes to bed plugged into his iPhone like a teenager. What were you listening to, Toony? *A Book at Bedtime*?"

"Pink Floyd, actually. Any snoring from you two?"

"Dunno," said Hayes. "I slept like a baby."

"I was out like a light," added Guise. "Mind you, Hayes wakes up strangely." The others were all ears. "Most people would say 'Mornin'' or just grunt. He says 'Job done!'"

"I do," agreed Hayes. "Well, when you've woke up, that's your top priority for the day done and dusted, innit? Plain sailin' after that. Job done. Job's a good 'un."

"What about Guisey?" asked McDonald, keen for his old friend not to escape any flack. "Any weird behaviour?"

"Well, not weird, exactly," started Hayes. Guise looked at him askance. "But by the time I got up, his washed socks were pegged up in the bathroom and the rest of his kit was already packed away in little stuff bags, neatly lined up on the bed. Bed already made too. Says he ain't been in the army, but not sure I believe him."

"McDonald spends a suspicious amount of time in the bathroom," said Toon. "What's he up to?"

Thankfully, before McDonald could answer the waitress arrived to take cooked breakfast orders.

McDonald: "Full Irish, please."

Toon: "Full Irish."

Hayes: "Full Irish."

Guise: "Nothing, thanks."

All eyes swung on him.

"Don't you like cooked breakfast?" asked McDonald, as though accusing Guise of being a closet goat-botherer.

"Yes," he replied. "But we'll be away from public loos this morning and I don't want to take the risk."

Captain Careful lives. The waitress having made a rapid retreat, Guise placed three pills on his empty breakfast plate.

"What are they?" asked McDonald.

"Two of them are food supplements."

Guffaws.

"Does it say sausage on one and bacon on the other?"

"Not that kind. They're for bones. Dodgy knees."

He was wasting his breath, though. They wouldn't be letting that one go.

While the boys weren't the only guests, their chance of finding out how any of the others had ended up here in paradise were scuppered by the alien presence (for a hotel's breakfast room) of a television. A huge television. Switched on. That the western world seems to have succumbed without resistance to an invasion of TV screens seems to have escaped the news media. The previous night half the occupants of Murphy's seemed to have been transfixed by the same outsized TV behind the bar, as though it were showing the first steps of humankind on the surface of Mars, when in fact it was showing Nottingham Forest losing at home to Brighton and Hove Albion. And here at breakfast time it was still switched on. It didn't even appear to be an Irish channel, which would at least have constituted some local interest, but a British one – which is to say that half the 'news' concerned the marital perturbations of Hollywood celebrities or the latest gang affiliations in the Westminster playground. With the volume being turned up too, the rest of the breakfast passed with those guests facing the

TV hypnotised by the alien presence and those with their backs to it staring at the pictures on the wall.

Incredibly, in the contest for MIPTAI 16 (Most Inappropriate Presence of Television in All Ireland, 2016), Murphy's Killarney was to win only a silver medal.

*

Having settled on a route some six kilometres south of Killarney, to Torc Waterfall via Muckross House, the foursome set off beside the main road out of town. Strung along both sides were guest house after guest house, hotel after hotel, many looking pretty new. One of the informative customers at the previous night's bars had said that "they went mad with building when that Celtic Tiger was here." Another claimed that Killarney and its environs boasted 40,000 beds for visitors. At the time the boys doubted it. In the cold light of day it seemed perfectly possible.

Having successfully steered the boys from Quorn to Killarney – and already a little weary of being chief map and leaflet carrier – Guise offered the job of today's navigator to Toon, who happily accepted. Both are map fiends, Guise coming at it from Geography teaching (resignation after three weeks, admittedly) and Toon from sailing (hence the 'Skipper' tag). While perusing the maps back in the bar, Toon had berated Guise A) for drawing on one map a bold felt-tip line marking their train route across Ireland and B) for folding the local map to fit a map case in a way that guaranteed holes in the corners. Beneath Guise's implacable exterior lay a slightly seething resentment. If seething can be slight.

Ten minutes out from Murphy's Bar and Toon was looking up at two signs and scratching his head. Guise couldn't conceal his delight.

"Lost already?"

"No. Well, not exactly. I just don't know which way to go."

"That's what I'd call lost."

"One sign points to Ross Castle and the other to Muckross House."

"Well, as we're aiming for Muckross House, why not follow that?"

"McDonald here thinks they may be the same place."

"With different names and different directions?" Guise wondered if the bright Atlantic sun had already got to his companions.

"Well, if you put it like that..."

They followed the sign to Muckross House. This took them along an exposed path parallel to the busy road and pretty soon not just multi-layered Toon but all four were casting off their outer clothes in the unseasonal morning heat. Eventually their path dived into trees to their right and across open fields to hug the banks of the lough. With the light breeze, dappled sunlight and occasionally swooping birds, it was indeed something like paradise.

"Isn't that a blue tit?" asked Guise.

"I hate birds," said Toon, as a dog and its owner approached. "Hate dogs too."

"Any animals you don't hate?"

Skipper mulled over this for a few seconds. "Humans," he said. "A few of them are all right." The 'lost' incident was clearly festering.

Everywhere were signs of rough weather just past: fallen branches, gouged furrows, sticks and broken reeds washed high above the current level of the lough, a tideless inland lake. At one point a rushing stream washed noisily under a footbridge before emptying into the lake.

"Anyone for Pooh Sticks?" asked McDonald.

For all Britons of a certain age no further explanation was needed. All except Hayes.

"How do we know which direction they'll float in?" asked the Councillor.

A few metres to their right the lough lay calm and, well, watery. None of the leaflets had mentioned the famous Drained Lakes of Killarney. Such was the disconnection between Hayes and the universal forces of nature revealed by his question that none of the others could think of a response. So he simply followed their lead. Within a minute each had selected his stick and was leaning over the parapet on the *upstream* side.

"Three, two, one... go!" shouted McDonald.

Four splashes, four scurries to the downstream side and three cheers: "There's mine!"

"Where's mine?" asked Guise.

While the others cheered on their respective vessels, Guise descended to the stream.

"It's disappeared. How could that be? Wait a minute. Here it comes. I'm nearly under the bridge..."

All other eyes, meanwhile, were focused many metres downstream

"Yes!" shouted McDonald the Pooh. "I win! I win!"

Indeed he had. This was clearly unfair: he'd played the game before. Surely that wasn't in the rules. Hotly discussing the details of a handicap in the next run, they hadn't noticed the rapid approach of a heavy-booted, expansively bearded man a few years older than them.

"Haffing fun, lads? Right marfelous veather, ay man?"

After they'd deciphered his odd accent, they learnt pretty rapidly (for he spoke pretty rapidly and without hesitation) that Bearded Man was a Sunderland-born German resident. You meet all sorts in Ireland. He was following in the footsteps of his parents who'd honeymooned here many honey moons ago, his father being a keen fiddler intent on picking up a few new tunes in the far west. Without so much as a pause for breath, the discourse switched from tax affairs to boat trips to investment tips to the poor state of Sunderland FC... and back again. Feeling an interruption might be needed to move things on before sundown, Guise asked him if he'd be so kind as to take their photo. Having duly obliged, Bearded Man seemed to have lost his drift and set off in the same direction as the boys were heading, though not before calling back a supplementary comment on the interest rates in Frankfurt. The whole exchange was to be strange precursor to a similar, but more extreme event, two days later.

At a much more leisurely pace than their new financial advisor, they set off in a vaguely Muckrossian direction. Before long the path split into two, one on each side of a low fence. Skipper Toon was undecided. While they mulled over their options, two young cyclists pulled up just a few metres away and began discussing their own options in German. (Could it have been a Bavarian bank holiday?) In his schoolboy German, Guise called across to them.

"*Sind Sie auch verloren?*" ('Are you lost too?' he claimed was the translation.)

Glaring at him as though he'd asked "Do you two fancy a bit of pedal action behind this bush?"', they re-mounted and shot off at some speed.

Toon chose the left path. After two minutes, they were all climbing over the fence back onto the right path. After another two they were diverting left again to what looked like a promising ruin, what turned out in fact to be Muckross Abbey.

By now the boys had wandered into Killarney National Park, Ireland's first national park, formed in the 1930s when the owners of the Muckross Estate donated it to the nation. What most visitors come to visit (or at least what most are delivered by their coaches to visit) is Muckross House, a Victorian pile built for the local MP. By that time, however, both Muckross Abbey and Ross Castle, on the other side of the lake, had already been around for about 500 years. While the castle was the ancestral home of the O'Donoghue clan, the abbey was home to an order of Franciscan friars. Nowadays, while not a complete ruin, it certainly shows its age – although the cloister surrounding a venerable yew tree is still in good shape.

Having predictably set off on a tour of the place in four different directions, the boys eventually re-grouped at His Highness's calling before a certain gravestone...

An hour later (half of which was taken up by Pooh Sticks Round 2 – another victory for the all-conquering McDonald, now widely suspected of dirty tricks), they rolled up at Muckross House, awash with coaches and tourists. 'Never pass a toilet' is a wise motto for men over sixty and sure enough all four headed for the loo. Or rather loos. With no pre-planning in place, all four emerged at different times from different exits and proceeded to wander off in completely different directions. After thirty mysterious minutes (*The Lost Half-Hour*, not a blockbuster, it has to be said), first Guise, then Hayes and then McDonald eventually found their way to the cacophonous cafeteria, where a queue longer than the Giant's Causeway and comprising several coachloads of Continental children barred their way to a simple lunch break. Navigating from the rear, Skipper Toon finally showed up too, to lead the hungry hobos out beyond the ha-ha and down to the lakeside, where peace and tranquillity once more prevailed.

Should you find yourself in these parts, Torc Waterfall is indeed recommended as a sight – and sound – to behold, but be prepared to experience the wonder with yet more hordes of visitors, for nearby lies another coach park. The boys did, however, benefit from the kindness of an American with a selfie stick, who offered to take another team shot. Not with the selfie stick, naturally. As is the way with people fond of equipment, especially up-to-date equipment, he couldn't help himself declaring "Hey, what you guys want is one of these!" McDonald showed no sign of recognising the irony.

An ambling return, including Pooh Sticks Round 3 – McDonald defeated: that's all that matters – finally delivered the famished quartet to the front of the cafeteria queue and a table of speedily scoffed sarnies. Seven miles covered, as estimated in old money by the map men, too knackered for conversions. A bus back to town for eight euros each was decided upon. This being Ireland, though, even that wasn't straightforward. The bus was due to leave the coach park at 3.15. At 3.10 a bus with no destination plate stood there, engine running. Guise approached the driver.

"Is this the bus to Killarney?"

"Yes and no."

"Yes *and* no?"

"This is *a* bus to Killarney, but it's not *the* bus to Killarney."

"Are you going to Killarney?"

"Yes."

"When?"

"Right now."

"How much?"

"Five euros each."

"We're in, lads."

Excellent ride, excellent views, no tickets.

*

Back at Murphy's, before the boys split up to do battle with the bathrooms, a plan had been hatched. This, at least, was progress. Tonight's tour of Killarney's hostelries would involve none visited the night before.

"Agreed."

"Meet downstairs in the bar in an hour," instructed McDonald, drinks monitor.

"But we drank here yesterday," said Hayes.

"Just do as I say."

So after three and a half pints at Murphy's (Captain Careful alternating pints with halves) and a pointless argument between Toon and McDonald about what constituted a high street, the foursome entered Charlie Foley's Bar. This brought the total number of customers there to four. Now some would immediately walk out of an empty pub, but McDonald was not one of the 'some': a pub's a pub for all that. Subsequent research established that this one was frequented by young persons, i.e. persons who don't emerge in the hours of daylight. Said research also threw up a five-star review stating:

> Oh my gosh the owner is such a doll, If I was'nt [sic] taken I would snatch him up move to killarny [sic] and have 20 of his kids. LOL.

Excuse me while I'm sic [sic]. Perhaps, to aid public awareness, all establishments serving liquor should be required by EU law to display an 'Expected Clientele' notice in their window, including citations relevant to the establishment:

> 'Maximum age: 30. Minimum tattoos on display: 1. Maximum tattoos on display: unlimited. Acceptable conversation: vacuous.'

> 'Minimum age: 50. Sex: females discouraged. Pets: physically ejected. Caps: cloth or none. Acceptable conversation: politics, sport, toilets.'

> 'Minimum age: 18. Maximum age: 40. Minimum age of mobile phone: 6 months. Acceptable conversation: mobile phones, relationships, hair styles, trouser width.'

> 'Minimum age: 1 day. Maximum age: 45. Sex: male adults allowed only if accompanied by children. Prams: the wider the better. Acceptable conversation: babies, dogs, *Strictly*, *Bake-Off*, particle accelerators.' (After all, some outstanding scientists are female.)

Having exhausted the scope of the young barman's early-evening conversation (a task of about thirty seconds), the boys retired with their pints to a secluded corner to break the unwritten rules of the bar and discuss politics among themselves. Ireland, what is it?

"A rebel state."

"An heroic republic, God bless 'em."

"An island."

"What was the question again?"

Having thankfully exhausted that topic before the locals arrived, Guise tried something more intellectual. Space, what is it?

"This, between my hands." (Toon held his hands about a foot apart.)

"The place beyond the stratosphere."

"Three dimensions."

"Space is Prince Charles's favourite girl band?"

"That's Three Degrees, oik."

"Something to be filled with beer."

He tried again. Time, what is it?

"What clocks measure."

"Another dimension."

"A herb."

"No, T-I-M-E, oik."

"Oh, dunno."

"A period in which to drink beer."

Message received. They moved on.

*

Round the corner in High Street (or, according to Toon, merely *a* high street) was Danny Mann's. This was a different kettle of stout altogether:

> Minimum age: 10. Maximum age: 80. Sex: two (or possibly three) widespread. Nationality: unlimited. Tattoos: none on display. Headgear: remove on entry. Music: live, middle-of-the-road. Tables: grab any that's free.

First to enter as usual, McDonald spotted one near the band (a would-be Sonny and Cher for the 21st century) and duly grabbed it, installing himself and Hayes. Toon, with the peripheral vision of a sailor in high seas, spotted one near the window and grabbed it, installing himself and Guise. While waiters pounced on each pair with menus and drinks orders, all four looked around for the missing pair. Exceeding even their own standards of disorientation, the boys had managed to get lost simply by entering a pub. Back in Quorn, along with three other navigationally challenged gentlemen, the four venture out on quarterly pub crawls within a train or bus ride of the village. They call themselves the Leicestershire Order of Social Travellers (LOST). On their last outing, to the local town – a mere ten minutes away – the leader, who'd spent the best part of a month researching the project, got completely lost within a minute of stepping off the bus.

After a brief stand-off and some hazardous semaphore, the two distant pairs in Danny Mann's opted for the window seats and settled down to the best plates of fish and chips on the tour. Watered down, surprisingly enough, by a few glasses of Guinness. Music in a pub is all very well, but if amplified it does tend to inhibit conversation, even inane conversation. So it was back to Murphy's, where a promising line from the barman on the evident need for counselling among most of his customers was once again interrupted by a band. A traditional Irish session – on this occasion guitar, fiddle and accordion – but once again unnecessarily amplified and therefore overpowering. Traditional in style, but not in effect.

The boys had soon had enough of this. Or, just possibly, having started at five o'clock, had had too much pop. Whatever, after the Carnegie of Quorn (Councillor Hayes), had unexpectedly presented each of the team with a 'Murphy's' tee-shirt (or, in the case of XXL McDonald, re-presented him with one that would fit), they retired. Tonight they'd made it to 10.15.

Just shadows of their former selves: the foursome at the bridge over the River Flesk, Killarney

The unmistakable silhouettes of McDonald and Toon as they try and work out where they are.

Paradise: Lough Leane, County Kerry.

The boys lean beside Lough Leane.

Striding purposefully onward from Muckross House.

Intense concentration at Pooh Sticks, Game 2.

Incontrovertible evidence of jiggerypokery by McDonald at Pooh Sticks.

You Have to Arrive Here to Get Here

Wednesday, Killarney to Dingle.

Though well ahead of the two slackers (Hayes and McDonald), Guise was only second to emerge the next morning.

"Your friend's already gone out into the rain," said the young woman on reception as he descended the stairs. "Where are you boys headed today now?"

"Oh, not far. Just to Dingle."

"Not faaar?" she said, mimicking his English pronunciation. "That'd be faaar enough for us here in Killarney."

There seems to be something about Guise's accent in particular that amuses the Irish. This wasn't the first time such gentle mimicry had broken out. Many years before, alone on the train from Dublin to Galway, Guise found himself sitting opposite someone who wanted to talk. Well, that would be just about any Irish rail passenger.

"It's a fine way to travel, isn't it?" asked the elderly man, in a strong Irish accent.

"Yes, I like trains too."

"There's something relaxing about it, wouldn't you say? You don't have a care, do you?"

"No, indeed."

"I do."

"Oh, I'm sorry," said Guise, putting on what he hoped was a sympathetic expression. "What is it?"

"A Ford Escort."

"Oh, a car!" said Guise loudly.

"Oh," responded the rest of the carriage, in unison. "A caaar!"

*

At Murphy's, the receptionist hadn't finished her interrogation.

"You'll be taking the train?"

"No, actually, we've opted for the bus."

"That'll be the Bus Éireann, will it?"

"Yes. Change at Tralee."

"Did you know there's a new private service that goes direct to Dingle? Cheaper too, they say. There's a leaflet here somewhere. Here it is. Now does it run today?"

"I don't know."

"I know you don't know. That's why I'm lookin' fer ya. Oh, no weekly schedule. I'll phone 'em. Oh, no phone number. Well, there you have it, sir. They'll hardly be gettin' many passengers, will they now? That Celtic Tiger's surely run off for good."

After another breakfast overlooked by the giant TV, but otherwise excellent, the four boys set off for the bus station, marked on the map next to the railway station where they'd arrived. Rolling up at the railway station, they couldn't help noticing the absence of anything bus-related. A bus, for example.

"You've got this wrong, Guise," said Skipper Toon. Was there in his tone a hint of mild cartographical revenge?

"I'll ask inside." He did.

"Yes, the bus station's right there, you see?" said the stationmaster, pointing to a clutch of coaches just beyond the station platform. Between the rail track and the buses, a distance of twenty metres at most, stood some high metal railings. Railings that said in no uncertain terms: 'Thou shalt not pass.'

"How do we get there?"

"Oh, you have to walk back into town, turn right and then come out again."

And he was right! Killarney's railway and bus stations are located literally side by side, but with no access between the two. Being from near Loughborough, the boys were familiar with bus-related insanity, but this surely took the transport biscuit. However paradisical Killarney may be, has it never occurred to the town council that one or two passengers arriving by public transport may be doing so in order to continue their journey elsewhere? Do the words 'Change at Killarney' mean nothing to them? The mystery was to remain unsolved, as with a bus to catch – and tickets to buy – the boys now had to hastily retrace their steps before leaving town on a parallel road.

*

Killarney bus station, though now temporarily short of buses (delayed by a diversion near Tralee), was filled with waiting passengers, some of them female and some of these alone. Promising territory for the Councillor. A smart-looking lady with white teeth and brown cowboy boots was sheltering from the drizzle. 'Gamine' was the way McDonald later described her. Hayes placed himself beside her and made his pitch.

"Miserable day, innit?"

"Sure is... hey, you ain't from round here, are you?"

For once, appearances hadn't deceived: she was from Texas. As the other three idled nonchalantly by – whether to learn from Hayes' chat-up technique or later criticise it wasn't clear – the Councillor interrogated her. She and her husband lived in a nearby village.

"Nice place?" enquired Hayes.

No comment. While they had the legal right of residence, this wasn't permanent.

"Oh dear," sympathised Hayes.

The bureaucracy was lengthy.

"Tut tut."

And proof of income virtually impossible to obtain. It was extremely unsettling.

"Never mind."

Just as Hayes was mulling over how to sit next to Gamine Lady on the bus to Tralee, a coach pulled in displaying 'Cork' above its windscreen. At this, she bid a rather hurried farewell to her would-be therapist and boarded it.

"Oh dear," said McDonald to Hayes.

"Tut tut," said Toon.

"Never mind," added Guise.

"She was definitely warming to me," opined the eternal optimist.

*

By the time the Number 40 to Tralee pulled in, few passengers were left and the boys were able to spread themselves and their bags around the rear few seats. Being furthest forward, Guise was nearest the other passengers and soon found himself in conversation with an Irish lad in his early twenties. They'd all noticed him at the bus station: a short chap in constant motion, eyes darting this way and that as though trying to identify a fast-moving butterfly. In the bus he was uneasy in his seat. Like all the Irish, it seems, he was keen to know where they were all from and where they were all going.

"The Dingle Peninsula today," said Guise.

"Oh, yes. Tralee, Brandon, Dingle, Ventry. I'm from there," said Uneasy Lad. His Irish accent came out in rapid-fire bursts.

"From where?"

"Cheltenham."

This answer didn't quite compute.

"Cheltenham?"

"Yes, Gloucestershire. I was born there. Could've been worse. Could've been a shit-hole like Tralee."

"Oh, I've never been there before. What's wrong with it?"

"It's a shit-hole." He paused, as though considering an explanation, but none was forthcoming. "Football stadium saving grace. Know what I mean?"

"Yes," said Guise. No, he thought.

"So me, I'm back to Cheltenham."

"What will you do there?"

It probably wasn't going to be anything in the tourist office.

"Oh, anything. Something." He paused again. "Anything."

They were both silent for a while. Then Uneasy Lad turned to Guise again.

"Don't mean to bother you," he said. "Enjoy the ride."

"You're not bothering me," Guise assured him, though guessed he might well have bothered others in his time.

As the outskirts of Tralee gathered along the roadside, it was clear that Uneasy Lad had a point. Industrial estates, carpet warehouses, drab modern housing...

"You see?" he said. "Like the Crawley of Ireland. A shit-hole."

It was raining again too. Scurrying into the bus station, the boys quickly confirmed that the 275 to Dingle had already gone and they faced two hours in the Crawley of Ireland. A damp trudge into the town centre did nothing to raise their spirits, especially as they were scheduled to stay overnight here on the way back. The highlight for Hayes and Toon was a local chap they stood next to in a bar and who had but one response to everything Hayes said.

"Miserable day out there, innit?"

"Ooh."

"Bet it's like this half the time, ain't it?"

"Oooh."

"Blimey this Guinness ain't 'alf cold."

"Ooooh."

"Well, we got a bus to catch. See ya."

"Oooooh!"

Maybe he was standing on Oooh Man's broken toe.

Reassembled at Tralee bus station, the others realised how lucky they were not to have appointed Hayes as chief navigator. Guise had reminded them all that they were catching the Number 275 to Dingle. As they waited, the Number 40 to Cork pulled in, easily identified by the large display declaring '40: Cork' in the windscreen.

"Come one, lads," said Hayes. "This'll be ours."

*

It would be hard to imagine an hour's bus journey more spectacular than that between Tralee and Dingle. As the grey streets of Tralee are left behind, you're soon cast onto the coast road, an arrow-straight line carved between the sheep-speckled slopes of the Slieve Mish Mountains to your left and the big skies over Tralee Bay to your right. As long as the road stays flat the sea remains nothing more than a thin blue line between the dark green fields and the Fenit shore beyond. But after Derrymore the road shifts a little up the slope and, as Tralee Bay turns into Brandon Bay, you begin to glimpse in the distance fainter but bigger headlands jutting out into the ocean. Finally, beyond a small, straggly community called Camp, you're suddenly hoisted up onto the shoulders of the heavy hills to be given a breathtaking view over an emerald patchwork sweeping down to a string of pure-white sand beside the sparkling blue waters of Brandon Bay. Farther out, between the pincers of Brandon Head and the Maharees, a misty horizon marks the start of the wild North Atlantic – and beyond the ocean lie the Americas.

Rocked in their seats as the bus driver swung around the hairpin bends, the boys looked first this way then that, calling over to Toon, his map spread across his lap, to identify what they were gawping at. By the time the bus had left the north coast behind and struck out across the spine of the peninsula, Toon and Guise had managed to convert the calm of the landscape into a matter for animated debate.

"Was Ireland glaciated?" asked Guise.

"No, I don't think so," suggested Toon. "Too far south."

"Well, these hills look glaciated to me."

"But the valleys aren't U-shaped enough."

"But surely that's a corrie up there."

By the magic of the internet, a geological map was brought to life on the screen of a smartphone, a map which, strange to tell, showed them both to be right. A big arrow pointing south-westwards from Ulster showed the direction of a huge ice sheet (advantage Guise), but much of the area that is now County Kerry was covered with the words 'Not widely glaciated' (advantage Toon). However, west of a line crossing the neck of the Dingle Peninsula, one small word popped up here and there: 'Corries' (advantage Guise). But corries are features of hilltops, not valleys. So where they sat at the altitude of the road had probably not been under a glacier, while where they were looking out of the window to the hills probably had. A draw. Game over.

*

At 5.25pm the Number 275 dropped the boys on Dingle Quay.

Sited at the head of a large natural harbour and protected by Ballymacadoyle Hill, from the prevailing south-westerlies and from seaward observation, Dingle developed as a defensive settlement and a port. Its Irish name is *Daingean Uí Chúis* ('Ó Cúis' stronghold), but it seems all the Irish-speaking locals call it *An Daingean* ('the stronghold').

Whatever its name, to the boys it looked perilously like another shot at paradise. Fishing boats and leisure craft rocked and creaked in the little inner harbour. Beyond this, Dingle Harbour itself – an area of about three square kilometres, almost entirely enclosed by hills, large and small – sparkled in the weak sun that had followed the rain. Facing this panorama was a small row of colourful cafes, bars and gift shops. Following Murphy's of Killarney, they were booked in for two nights at Murphy's of Dingle. It turned out there were two of them. As if completely ignorant of each other's existence, there they stood, side by side. Having assured themselves they weren't seeing double, two boys were despatched into one and two into the other. A minute later they all emerged onto the pavement.

"It's this one," said Guise from left-hand Murphy's.

After a simple check-in by a young man of few words, but whose physique said 'Any trouble and you'll have me to answer to', the foursome soon emerged back on Dingle Quay. Within a minute four had become three as Skipper Toon was magnetically drawn to the clutch of yachts in the western harbour. Within another, three had become two as His Highness, noticing that it was after six and he hadn't got a pint glass in his hand, dived into the Marina (a bar, not a watery haven). Captain Careful and the Councillor looked at each other and at the re-gathering clouds.

"When in Spain..." said Hayes, enigmatically.

Guessing at a slight Mediterranean confusion, Guise suggested: "... do as the Romans do?"

"Spot on."

With McDonald already supping and Hayes' and Guise's orders on the way, it was left to Toon, his maritime juices now flowing, to confuse the barmaid.

"You got any roasted peanuts?"

"No."

"Salted peanuts?"

"No."

"Crisps?"

"No. We've got Tatoes."

"No crisps?"

"Tatoes are crisps."

"No, crisps are made from potatoes."

"I know that. Do you want some or not?"

"What?"

"Tatoes!"

"I want crisps if you've got some."

She placed a packet of crisps on the bar. It said 'Tatoes' on the front.

"You call crisps Tatoes?" asked Toon.

"Yes."

"What do you call peanuts?"

"Peanuts."

"And you haven't got any?"

"No."

"I'll have some Tatoes then."

Game, set and match to the barmaid.

*

Downtown Dingle has just five streets. And yet, furnished with clear directions to the next pub from Tatoes Barmaid, the boys still managed to spend half an hour wandering around the tiny town like lost children. Uneasy Lad on the bus had recommended *An Droichead Beag* and both he and the barmaid had used that most ominous phrase among direction-givers: 'You can't miss it'. Captain Careful had remembered the spelling but illogically put his faith in a street map that didn't have it marked. His Highness, having paid especially close attention to the barmaid, was soon cursing her very existence as he marched hither and thither without success. With the sea in his nostrils, Skipper simply roamed randomly around ToonWorld. Ever ready to engage with human life, the Councillor had asked the advice of an old chap with an unsteady gait – advice that was unsurprisingly tricky to obtain since Hayes, of course, had no idea of the name of the pub. Eventually – and simply by dint of walking every inch of Dingle – one by one they fell across *An Droichead Beag*. It means 'the little bridge', is bright yellow and indeed you couldn't miss it if you tried.

Last in – and only there at all because he'd spied in the distance an exhausted Captain Careful diving through the door – came the Councillor. He joined the others at the bar.

"I thought I'd never drink again," he panted.

"You boys look worn out," commented the young barmaid. "Where are you from?"

"Leicestershire."

"Have you walked all the way then?"

With other customers few and far between, these were the opening salvoes of a long and enlightening conversation. For the Irish, it seems, the next best thing to hearing the sound of someone's voice is to hear the sound of your own.

"You'll be doing Slea Head Drive?"

74

"Will we?"

"You will."

"We haven't got a car."

"You'll be getting a taxi. You'll go to Coumeenole Bay."

"Will we?"

"Everyone does. It's where they shot *Ryan's Daughter*. You'll have seen the fillum?"

McDonald: "Yes."

Guise: "No."

Toon: "Don't know."

Hayes: "Brian who?"

Chatty Barmaid: "Ryan."

Hayes: "They shot him?"

And so, as the Guinnesses went down, the conversation – like so many in Ireland – wavered along the boundary between the intelligible and the absurd. Like a painting by Salvador Dalí.

"Around Slea Head," continued Chatty Barmaid, "you won't understand them. They only speak Irish."

"They do?"

"No, of course not. But some accents are strong. Did you know only Irish *men* speak with a strong accent? The women don't [she said in a strong accent]. Now when the Celtic Tiger came there was too much building of those holiday homes. Then we had the recession and values halved. 'Would you be better payin' rent?' we asked ourselves. But dat's like trowing money on da fire. Sure the EU was a benefit to Ireland, but now we can't afford to leave."

Best at occasionally interrupting her stream of consciousness was McDonald.

"Is your accent local?"

"Oh yes, I'm from round here."

"Do you like it?"

"You know, I do. It's quiet. The Dingle Peninsula, it's like a dead end. You have to arrive here to get here."

And no one could argue with that.

*

Next up was a bar into which the Councillor had stuck his head during the Great Wander Around and which he reckoned was up their street. He was right. It was called Curran's.

The layout was simple, but it was one which none of them had ever seen before... until McDonald remembered he'd been in a similar one before... in fact almost identical to this one... in fact this one!

"You've been to Dingle before?" asked Guise.

"Yes."

"And you didn't mention it?"

"It's all a bit of a haze."

"Yes?" asked Hayes.

Now with pints in their hands, however, the others were busy taking in their surroundings.

The tall, narrow room of Curran's was home to a peculiarly Irish version of schizophrenia. On the right was a well-worn but polished wooden bar hosting the usual restricted offering of Guinness and not much else, while behind this rose half a dozen shelves loaded with bottles of miscellaneous spirits, plus a scattering of black-and-white photographs of old film stars such as Robert Mitchum. So far, so standard; but a hint of the business's *alter ego* was given by the surprising presence on the shelves of more hats than could be accounted for by the seven or eight bare-headed customers.

However, on the left, while the physical layout was the same, the bar was not a bar, the people behind were not serving and the shelves rising to the ceiling contained no alcohol at all. The bar appeared to be a counter, the people customers and the contents... well, there were more hats, there were Wellington boots, there were ties and there was row upon row of boxes that might have contained, well, anything. Back in the normal world this was what we would call a shop.

As the boys had entered, the locals had spread to the margins as though washed back by four large pebbles dropped into a pool. They were now eagerly observing. Perhaps this was their entertainment for the evening: watching the reaction of new arrivals to the strange surroundings. The Councillor duly obliged.

"I'd like to buy one of those caps, please" he announced to the barman, who directed him to a tall man whom the boys had taken to be another customer.

"The Dingle-pattern cap?" said the tall man, taking down one with a curvy peak and a pimple on top.

"If you say so, squire."

"What's your head size, sor?"

"Small."

"Let me measure it now. Why, you're normal."

"'Ear that, lads? I'm normal!"

They were not convinced.

So pleased was Hayes by the comfort of his new hat that he bought a second. So pleased was he with the second that he asked for a bag and a receipt. The description on the receipt was not 'Two caps' but 'Cap fitted', payment clearly being not for the item itself but for the personal service. Moreover, the receipt's heading offered some clues as to the contents of the mystery boxes:

James Curran
GENERAL MERCHANTS / PUBLICAN
Agents for Red Mills Dog & Horse Feed & Tenderleen Horse Feed
Coal & Briquettes

No unusual smells, however, emanated from the left-hand shelves.

While the Councillor had been conducting his transaction, His Highness had been fraternising with the customers, amongst whom he'd discerned an accent that was clearly not local. It belonged to a short, distinguished-looking gentleman with a neat grey beard on his chin and a twinkle in his eye. He wore a felt hat at a jaunty angle, a white collarless shirt and, of all things, a cravat.

"No," he admitted, when challenged, "I'm from London. Not the posh part, o' course."

"When did you leave?" asked McDonald.

"Oh, it'd be around 1970."

"Did you know the Krays?"

Not the obvious next question for most people, but for McDonald, though born and bred in Leicestershire, the violent post-war days of the East End of London held a strange fascination. It turned out that Bert (for such was Cravat Man's name) had indeed encountered one or two dodgy characters in his time and he and McDonald spent a happy ten minutes discussing the thumb-screwing, limb-severing, concrete-booting days of yore. After Toon and Guise had been included in the jolly old natter, McDonald eventually steered the subject matter back to Dingle.

"So what are you doing here, Bert?"

"Oh, I came here for the filming, you know."

"What filming?"

"*Ryan's Daughter.*"

"Were you an actor?" asked Guise, before realising the potential for insult in the tense. "I mean, *are* you an actor?"

The idea seemed to amuse Bert.

"No, I left that to Bob." He nodded at the photograph of Robert Mitchum. "I was an electrician on the set. Liked the place. Never left."

"Do you mind us asking how old you are?" asked McDonald.

"I'm ninety-two," said Bert.

After another round of drinks, including one for Bert, the boys eventually bid farewell to Curran's, surely a classic among Irish bars. As they bundled through the narrow doors, another of the locals whispered in McDonald's ear.

"Bert's a mere eighty-nine," he said.

*

By now the boys' stomachs were reminding them that since breakfast they'd had only a snack at a Tralee coffee bar. Back to the quay, the Dingle Bay Hotel and a table by the window. By the time they'd refilled with solids as well as more liquids, the bar was emptying. Eventually the only other table occupied was the one next to theirs, where a middle-aged couple were attacking two burgers about the size of small caravans.

According to census data, about forty million Americans claim Irish heritage, which is about seven times as many as the current population of Ireland, and so it wasn't surprising that Dingle was crawling with them. However, there are two types of Americans: those who stay in America and those who travel; and, as anyone who's met both will know, they're as different as chalk and chowder. So the travelling Americans at the next table were not only quiet, but well-informed and well-spoken. They were from Seattle. Once a conversation with the boys' table had begun, McDonald, as usual, waded right in.

"So what do you two think of Donald Trump? I've just come back from New York and the folks there were pretty embarrassed by him."

"Well, let me say this," said the woman. "I've been a lapsed Catholic for many years, but I'm now back in church prayin' it won't happen."

No disagreement there then, so McDonald tried a different tack.

"You've probably heard us arguing about the EU referendum in Britain. What do you think?"

"Oh, it's nothing to do with us. I try and avoid the subject. We like England though, and of course Ireland is something special."

At this her husband seemed to awake from a reverie.

"I've noticed," he said, "that there's a lot of wind in the west of Ireland. But you know what?" They didn't. "I ain't seen a single wind turbine. Now, I happen to be in the wind business and I have to say I find this odd."

The subject of energy also energised Toon, who'd spent the last few years in another – you might say a competitive – aspect of the business. He declared his hand to the wind man.

"Really?" he said. "Yes, we certainly like Ireland."

No controversy to be had there either.

Well, perhaps there'd been enough arguments for one day and in any case it was getting late. On this third day of the tour the boys had, to their own surprise, managed to stay up till a record-breaking eleven o'clock. Dirty stop-outs.

The mystery that is Killarney's bus and railway stations -- and ne'er the twain shall meet.

Between Killarney and Dingle, it's all too much for Skipper Toon

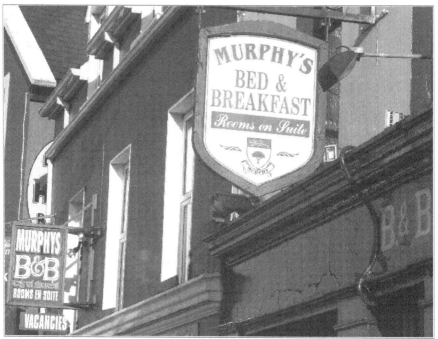

Is every B&B in County Kerry named Murphy's?

Watch out, Dingle -- the boys are in town.

In the Marina Inn the loos are so good they named them twice.

In Curran's Bar, McDonald and Toon get wiring tips from Bert, the electrician on 'Ryan's Daughter'.

Other Peninsulas Are Available

Thursday, Dingle Peninsula.

Another town, another Murphy's breakfast. This one, served and supervised by the well-built youth who'd checked them in, passed without incident (and, thankfully, without TV) until a lady emerging from the kitchen spotted something amiss.

"You boys'll be wanting to sit together," she said, tut-tutting. They sat at two neighbouring tables for two.

"No, we're fine," said Toon.

"No, you're not."

And she proceeded to push the table at which Guise and Hayes were eating towards the other one. Quite firmly and without warning. As his bowl of Rice Krispies disappeared, Guise was left spooning fresh air. Oblivious to the effect of her sudden horizontal displacement, but still tut-tutting, the lady promptly left the room.

This was to be their main walking day. The logistics of a six-day journey had been woven by Captain Careful to place them close to dramatic coastal scenery on one of just two days a week when a service bus could transport them to it and later return the weary walkers back to Dingle. When, the previous day, he'd mentioned the early bus time, McDonald had noticed that it would have meant missing his cooked breakfast.

"Are you mad?" he'd asked Guise, as though the latter had suggested to a drowning man that he let go of that log. "Aren't there taxis?"

And so after breakfast the four presented themselves at the Tourist Office on the quay, where a lady was happy to order them one. Being between eighteen and eighty and quite attractive, she naturally found herself the object of the Councillor's first attempt of the day. Perhaps he'd strike lucky. After all, he'd just received a text from a lady friend back in England that read: 'It's Day 3, David. Time to turn your pants inside out!'.

"I'm not from raand 'ere," he said to the lady in the Tourist Office, to her evident lack of surprise. "Where are we on this map?"

He was referring to a large map of Ireland affixed to the counter.

"We'll be here on the Dingle Peninsula in beautiful County Kerry."

"What are these four colours?" he asked, moving closer.

"Those," she explained, standing her ground, "are the four provinces of Ireland: Munster, where we are, Leinster, Connacht and Ulster."

"Is that the Midlands?"

She looked askance at Hayes.

"No. Ulster's clearly in the north. The clue's in the name, sir: *Northern Ireland.*"

James Curran, the hat man, was clearly not the only one in Dingle to have the measure of the Councillor.

"What's this down here then?" he asked, choosing an area of the map that would involve her leaning towards him.

"That'll be County Cork. Also very beautiful, sir, but in a sense our rivals."

"And which would you say is the most beautiful part of Ireland?" he asked, looking directly into the hazel depth of her eyes.

"Well, that'd be the Dingle Peninsula, sir. But other peninsulas are available. And," she added, with a glance over her shoulder, "that'll be your taxi."

Climbing into the back of the taxi, the Councillor gave McDonald and Guise his verdict: "She was definitely warming to me."

Toon, meanwhile, was hovering outside, patting his pockets.

"Can't find my wallet," he said. "I'll nip back to the digs. You'll have to wait."

On double yellow lines, as it happened, but their driver seemed pretty relaxed about things. At least that's what the others inferred from the tone of his words, even though they couldn't decipher a single one. With Toon and wallet happily reunited, they eventually set off and were soon passing through more spectacular scenery as they skirted Smerwick Harbour, with its white sands and rugged cliffs. As usual, Guise had been allocated the front seat and the job of conversing with the driver.

"Could you drop us here at this beach near Clogher?" he asked on a straight stretch of road and pointing at the map on his knee.

"Ah, daa diddle urdu an a Clogher an been," muttered the driver. It didn't seem to be Irish, but bore no recognisable connection to English either.

"Thanks," said Guise, working on sound rather than content. "Here's Ballyferriter, where we hope to end up. If you give me your number, I might ring you later."

"Manny murger um Ballyferriter," he replied, passing Guise a business card. "Midge da venture an purdle menta morda."

"Jolly good. Thanks."

After about ten minutes, during which the lanes had become narrower and narrower, they descended slowly to a tiny inlet where the road finally ran out completely. Before them the ocean poked a calm patch of blue around the headland until it touched the sands of a deserted little beach. This was Clogher Bay.

Guise paid the driver.

"Thanks," he said. "Maybe see you later."

"Ah, peddy doodle tha woon it."

*

Having taken in the air and their surroundings, the boys turned to Captain Careful. Trying to keep his badly folded map from Toon's critical gaze, Guise pointed back inland.

"We go back up the lane," he said, "and then pick up the coast road after about a mile.

"But there's a coast path here," said Toon. "It's marked 'The Dingle Way'."

Map Wars 2.

"According to the map, it just goes round in a circle and comes back here." When map and reality vary, Guise's always retains his faith in the map. Toon, however, had already set off up the cliff. "Oh, all right," said Guise.

And this time Toon was right. As they walked up over the green, spongy fields, they were treated to a spectacular and ever-widening panorama. Over to the south, beyond the bay, rose Clogher Head, mottled grey and green in the morning sunshine. Just behind it, but invisible from here, lay Dunmore Head, the westernmost point of the Irish mainland. Out to sea a rocky outcrop slowly transformed, as the boys walked further northwards, into the shape of a sleeping giant: this was Inishtooskert, the outermost of the uninhabited Blasket Islands. To the north the scenery was, if anything, even more dramatic. From the air the peninsula here forms the shape of a huge anvil-headed shark surging out to sea in the general direction of Greenland. This is Sybil Head, with the hills known as The Three Sisters to the north-east and, to the south-east, Sybil Point. Looking out to Sybil Point, the boys were unsure whether what they saw was something man-made or entirely natural. The craggy profile appeared to have been hewn into a series of giant-sized steps leading down to the sea, from where after barely fifty metres the steps rose again, scaled for even greater feet, to form an islet that looked like a piece of the giant's castle hurled down from the battlements.

But even this wasn't what Toon was training his binoculars on. Tracing a wavy white line up to the ridge of Sybil Head was a newly built track and up the track trundled a short convoy of articulated trucks, as though headed for a remote motorway service area but actually headed for a completely incongruous construction site, complete with cranes and scaffolding, that sat astride the ridge. What it appeared to be building was a collection of three or four huge towers, rather like a cruet set for the Giant of Sybil Head.

Toon confirmed what they'd all guessed: "It's the set for the next *Star Wars*."

According to a waitress at a Dingle cafe they were due to start shooting *Star Wars 8* in three weeks' time. None of them were fans.

"I saw the last one," said Guise, "but it didn't make any sense as I hadn't seen any of the others. It finished with a scene on Skellig Michael, which is round here somewhere, with some ancient ruins built like beehives. Those towers must be reproductions for the next one."

As they were walking along, gazing into the distance, none of them had noticed even stranger things nearer to hand. Down toward the shore, just beyond a waterfall, lay a small area of level grass and on this patch sat two figures, cross-legged and probably female. They were both facing directly across to the film set on the hill opposite and here's the thing: they were bowing up and down, repeatedly and in unison. Without a break and without a word.

"Are they Muslims?" whispered Hayes.

"More like Jedi," hissed McDonald.

And indeed, after quietly staring for a minute or two, the boys decided that was the most likely explanation. Film buffs are weird enough, *Star Wars* buffs weirder than most. Was this the time to tap them on the shoulder and ask them what it's all about? Probably not. The boys sneaked away, feeling just that bit saner.

In any case, Toon and Guise had Map Wars 3 to consider. Sheltering the map case from sun and wind, they both peered at the tiny print and even tinier symbols.

"Well, it's clear where we are," said Guise. "Here's the waterfall."

"So why don't we just carry on along the top of these cliffs?"

"Well, on the map the path heads back to the road."

"But in front of our eyes it carries on by the coast. Must be an old map."

"Fair enough."

"Hang on a minute."

Before Guise knew what was going on, young Toon had bounded ahead and down onto the rocks, where he proceeded to deliver to his audience of two (Hayes and McDonald) a brief lecture on the nature of shale, its origins and properties, breaking bits of the peninsula off as he did so. While he just about held the attention of his audience, Guise still puzzled over the mysteriously uninformative map, before shrugging his shoulders and following the others.

After a few easy minutes, things became a little complicated as they found themselves mincing along an ever-narrower strip of uneven ground between a barbed-wire fence and an ominous drop to the bone-shattering rocks below. One by one they carefully scaled the fence, only to find themselves in what looked like a field of harmless grass, but turned out to be a field of mud. Ever-deepening, cloying mud. Perhaps sensing defeat in Map Wars 3, Toon was clearly the nimblest and so McDonald and Guise followed his lead over a series of tufts to the left. Hayes, meanwhile – and for no evident reason – had set out to the right, where he first strode, then squelched and finally lurched his way into a muddy cul-de-sac. As the others watched, he managed to get further into trouble by clambering over more barbed wire which placed him neatly in a barbed-wire sandwich. What could have been the last nail in the Councillor's coffin would have been the appearance at this stage of a slavering hound bounding towards his helplessly corralled victim. 'Local councillor meets sticky end in deepest Ireland' would have read the headline in the *Loughborough Echo*. Fortunately all remained quiet as, bit by bit, Hayes returned to civilisation in the form of a nearby farm track where he spent the next ten minutes washing the mud from his lower limbs in a cattle trough before re-joining the others as though nothing had happened.

*

Back on *terra firma*, they finally headed inland along the winding lanes that encircled the scattered village of Ballyferriter. This is not, alas, where someone used to catch ferrets for use in classical dance (such practice being strictly illegal nowadays of course), but simply the townland ('*Bally*') of someone named Ferriter. The roads were not as quiet as they'd expected.

While Toon gave directions to an Italian couple in a car (making that the sixth nationality they'd come across after less than twenty-four hours on the Dingle Peninsula), the others went over to chat with a man hammering a stake into a hedgerow. He turned out to be English and, hearing their accents, became quite talkative and ended up inviting the four of them to call in at his house 'just over there' for a cuppa. They were later to remind Guise that it was he who actually said 'Yes'.

"I'll put the kettle on then," confirmed the hammerer.

Before they turned in at the collection of buildings he'd indicated, McDonald suggested they didn't really have time for social chit-chat, but Guise's argument that it would be rude to decline won the day. By the time they'd emerged about an hour later, Guise had already thrown in the towel.

"Did I tell you I was in aeronautics?" asked their host after carrying in a tray with four cups and a cafetière.

"No," said Guise. It would be the last word any of the boys would speak for the next fifteen minutes.

"Well," he started, "it was on the old XX14s, you know. Jolly fine piece of equipment. Twelve widgets, not ten of course. Positive torque, backward spliced. Responsible for the holes myself. Seventeen millimetre, I think. No, that was the XX13, surely. Yes, silly me, nineteen mil on the XX14... Rum office altogether, Wokingham [he changed subjects without changing gear]. Better off doing the tricky work at St Albans, of course. Wouldn't listen to me though, would they?..."

As no seats were available in the room, the boys were standing at awkward angles while listening to the monologue. Pretty soon all were shifting their weight regularly from leg to leg.

"Sports, though?" he droned on unprompted, but as smoothly as an XX14. "I should say so. Cricket, soccer, boxing... made men of us. Some were already men of course. Old Bandemann must have been pushing seventy but still strong as an ox. Worked on the PF70s back in the days when they were positively spliced, forwardly torqued, abstractly painted, fearlessly badgered, what?"

"What?" responded Guise, finding himself suddenly in the badger's gaze, as it were. "Coffee? Before it gets cold?"

The other three breathed a sigh of joyous relief at this sudden hint of progress. While Guise poured the coffee and handed it out, The Dingle Droner slowed the flow of his stream of consciousness, but it turned out to be just a temporary blockage, for soon the waters broke again.

"Wind tunnels, now there's a thing. Whole kit and caboodle goes in of course. Comes out in a hell of a state. Brackets scorched, sprockets deflowered, wodgets completely wurdled. All down to the adjustable holes in the gibbet-arm. Should be nineteen mil, like on the XX14. Did I tell you about the XX14?..."

After the boys had loudly placed their cups back on the tray, a sort of bid for freedom was made. Coats and boots were put back on, bags swung, apologies offered. But even as three of them had successfully made it to the road, Hayes was detained by showing unwise interest in the left-hand thread of the forty-eight-watt digit-throoper and was finally released only when Mrs Droner came out to lead her husband by the arm and back into the house.

"Maybe the old fellow never sees anyone," suggested McDonald, as they once more strode the happy strides of liberty.

"If he does," opined Toon, "he only sees them once."

After a brief stroll along Ballyferriter Beach, they straggled one by one into the welcome shade of one of the little village's several bars. Four soups, three Murphys and two dried socks later, they were in another taxi and headed back to Dingle. (Captain Careful doesn't imbibe at lunchtimes and Skipper Toon had decided to clean his boots in the ocean... while still wearing them.) Being uncertain of deciphering the mumblings of their previous driver over the phone, Guise had suggested the barman be challenged to find a local taxi for a better price. This he'd done with alacrity and a well-earned tip.

They'd walked about eight kilometres, but this wasn't enough for rugged, handsome, other-worldly Skipper Toon. Back in Dingle, as the old folks creaked their way upstairs for showers and naps, he pushed on eastward to pull in an extra four clicks (as the professional hard men say) by tramping out to the edge of the harbour and back again.

*

Another evening in Dingle and so many pubs to choose from. His Highness, though, was up to the task. On an earlier stroll he'd identified two more that bore an uncanny resemblance to the eclectic Curran's and recommended these to his loyal subjects. Dick Mack's was first, followed a pint later by Foxy John's. McDonald was right. Though the rears of these establishments were quite different – indeed characterful in their own ways – the main bars were of the same layout as Curran's. Licensed bar on one side, shop – or apparent shop – on the other. One was an ironmonger's, the other... actually, on later enquiry, none of the boys could remember what they sold. They all seemed to blur into one.

One venue was certainly distinguished by yet another attempted chat-up by the Councillor. A young girl, no older than her early twenties and from Lincolnshire it turned out, was carefully packing a series of leather belts into a bag on the shop side. (Maybe that's what they sold.) Feigning interest in leather accessories, Hayes waded in and, he later claimed, was doing pretty well until Guise, oblivious to his friend's steady progress, made it a threesome. She soon made her excuses and left.

"What was all that about Sleaford?" asked Hayes. "I was doin' all right, I'd even turned the subject round to leather trousers, when you come out with the landscape of the Fens and the history of Sleaford."

"Sleaford's not in the Fens."

"Well, there you are then. She was shocked by your poor geography."

Actually, not so long ago she wouldn't even have been permitted in that part of the bar. Just inside the front door of each of the three traditional bar-shops they'd visited was another, smaller doorway. This led to the snug. Unlike the snugs seen in many British pubs, these were originally reserved for two categories of people that were only half-allowed into the premises: women and priests. How times change.

*

After a quick bite to eat in the other Murphy's, the boys sauntered along the quayside for a last pint in John Benny's where half a dozen drinkers were leaning with their backs on the bar watching football on the television opposite. The boys joined them.

It was a just a Europa League quarter-final. Oh, Liverpool are playing.

May as well watch for a few minutes. Oh, it's the second half and they're already 0-2 down to Dortmund, 1-3 on aggregate – Liverpool are on the way out. Drink up, lads. Mm, good goal by Origi. 1-2. Muttering in German from the couple behind them. (Seven nationalities in Dingle.) Could be interesting. Another half? Ah, 1-3. 'Ja!' from behind. Well, we've ordered our drinks now. A few minutes passed. Liverpool aren't coming back from this. Time to go, lads. Coutinho, bang! 2-3. Hm. Twenty-five minutes to go. Four pints? Ten minutes later and another Liverpool goal. 'Scheisse' from behind. 3-3. Game on! Having heard the cheers from the streets, more people drift in. Nervous sips. Klopp's used all his subs. Ninety minutes. Good effort from Liverpool, but they're not going to make it. Ninety-one minutes. Milner down the right, crosses, Lovren, shoots. Goaaaaal! 4-3!! Kop and Klopp go beserk. Beer is spilt in Dingle. Final whistle. Blimey.

"*Entschuldigung* (Sorry)," said Guise to the German couple, slumped on the bar. They raised their heads and gave him a look suggesting he'd accused them of illegal goat-sexing. Maybe he had. Maybe his German isn't as good as he claimed.

Anyway, Klopp and Co had managed to keep the weary walkers up to an almost creditable 10.20.

The Mystery of the Moving Table. Let r1 = Location of Rice Krispies at Time t1...

The business end of the Dingle Peninsula, on a map torn from the hands of a passing pirate.

This is what we came for! Three of the boys stride north from Clogher Beach. (The fourth is holding the camera.)

The craggy coastline at Sybil Point.

"Now these," said Professor Toon, "are what we in the trade call rocks."

Councillor Hayes sorts himself out after a small adventure.

Three weeks to filming on the set for Star Wars 8.

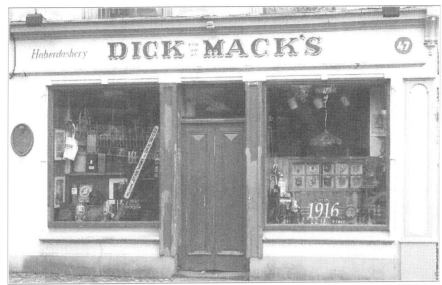

One of Dingle's traditional bar-cum-shops. Some reference to 1916 seemed to be obligatory.

For the Fifth Floor, Press Four

Friday, Dingle to Tralee.

Another breakfast, another American family digging up Irish roots. At least, the boys guessed it was some kind of family, though the question of the exact relationships between Marty and Laurie from Colorado and Peggy from Minnesota was to provide fertile ground for later speculation. (The others only just managed to stop the Councillor from drawing diagrams.) Peggy in particular seemed to have latched onto the concept of English banter pretty fast. On hearing that a book might come from the boys' short trip, she immediately offered some ideas for the title:

"Clueless in Dingle?"
"How did you know we're clueless?"
"Three Men and an Ass?"
"Which one's the ass?"

Grateful for such subtle suggestions, they promised Peggy a mention –

and here it is.

*

The weather, which had been almost Mediterranean out at Ballyferriter, had turned cooler. As they emerged from the B&B with a last morning to kill in Dingle, a breezy shower blew in. The official term for the day's forecast was 'iffy', but a boat trip around the harbour – with a specific objective – had been mooted.

"Now," announced His Highness, "I'm not a quitter in any shape or form. But I'm not going out to sea if it's raining."

"For which shape of quitter is that not quitting?" asked Captain Careful, adopting an uncharacteristically reckless stance.

"And anyway," added the Councillor, "I don't think a spin round the harbour actually counts as 'out to sea', does it Skip?"

But Skipper Toon was nowhere to be seen. Not quite true. A lone human of Toon-like form was to be spied through the drizzle in the far distance, snooping about the sloops at the western extremity of the quay. In terms of maritime meteorological tolerance, McDonald and Toon are at different ends of the mainbrace, as it were: as far as the Skipper's concerned, the rougher the better. But as he returned to the quayside shelter where the others were considering their options, he carried the hunched shoulders of a thwarted mariner.

"No yachts to be hired here," he said.

"Bit odd," suggested Guise. "I'd have thought it was prime yacht-hiring territory."

"Seems people either own them or come round from Kinsale. Anyway, it's no go."

That left a choice of two vessels, the decision between which took only about an hour of pointless blathering, by which time it had stopped raining and McDonald was testing out his sea legs. As they awaited departure, Skipper Toon told the others of a sailing experience further north on these wild western shores of the British Isles.

"Off the coast of Scotland between the islands of Scarba and Jura," he started, stroking his newly grown stubble for extra effect, "lies the narrow sound of Corryvreckan. The pilot books warn you to stay away, except at slack water and only if absolutely necessary. When the tide's ebbing, you see, it retreats faster than the sound allows the water to flow through it, leaving a difference in the water level of over a metre, effectively a waterfall. To add to the disturbance there's a large standing rock at some depth below the surface. Well, it was slack water, so we decided to give it a go."

"Even though it wasn't absolutely necessary," interrupted Captain Careful.

"Technically, no. Well, when we entered the sound, although there was no apparent tide flowing, there were whirlpools everywhere, kicking the yacht first to one side, then the other. We were motoring of course, but it was as though the sea was trying to take away control of the boat. Pretty scary stuff."

"Any whirlpools round here?" asked McDonald.

"Not as far as I'm aware. Anyway, we're not even going out of the harbour!"

*

It's barely two kilometres from the quayside to the narrow passage where Dingle Harbour opens out into Dingle Bay and it was here that both boats, each with about a dozen passengers, steered what to an observer would have looked like the course of either aggressors or madmen. To and fro they tacked, like a pair of flamenco dancers, until a crackle on the radio of the boat the boys had chosen told them that the other had spotted their joint prey. Actually, 'prey' is a completely inappropriate metaphor, since for all parties the experience was to be nothing but joy.

Back in the early 1980s, as Ireland's Johnny Logan couldn't stop winning the Eurovision Song Contest, a bottlenose dolphin wandered into the environs of Dingle. (There's no evidence that it was attracted by the saccharin songs of the Celtic crooner, but who knows?) It was male and is thought to have arrived, so said the jolly and informative guide on the lads' boat, with a female, who soon died. Anyway, lovelorn or not, the dolphin seems to have taken to Dingle and has never left.

Exactly what keeps him here is uncertain, but one thing was sure: riding the bow waves between a pair of chugging boats gave him a hell of a buzz that morning. Over and over again he surfaced next to this vessel or that, to port or starboard, heading north or south... although, stressed the guide, no morsels are offered and none should be offered: he seems to live almost entirely off the local stock of a needle-shaped fish called a garfish. Over the years many observers have studied the dolphin and one once commented that she was sharing the waters with a real 'fun guy'. (Yes, she was North American.) The name stuck and he's nowadays known, on hundreds of mugs, tee-shirts and tea-towels, as 'Fungie', the Dingle Dolphin. 'Dougal' would have completed the alliteration, but never mind. Perhaps the most interesting of the many little snippets about Fungie that the guide shared was that whenever a school of dolphins wanders into the bay, as they occasionally do, Fungie heads for the deepest corner of his home waters that he can find, hiding till they wander off again, unaware of his existence.

Duly chilled and wind-blown, the boys spent their last half-hour in Dingle warming their cockles in *An Cupán Tae* cafe, whose background entertainment of choice was Radio Kerry: 'Your Voice in the Kingdom'. The voice that day set the light-hearted tone that everyone loves to hear from local radio by running through the gruesome details of murders and suicides in the Italian Versace family. A jolly old departure from Dingle then.

*

After another scenic, but uneventful, ride on the 275 bus, the boys checked into Tralee's Townhouse B&B. Having noted when he'd briefly called in two days before that the receptionist was somewhat 'adjacent', Guise left the check-in to Skipper Toon.

"Here are your keys," said the local. "You're all on the fifth floor, so when you get in the lift, press number four."

A minute later they were back at Reception.

"The lift's full of laundry," said Toon.

"Well, you'll have to walk up the stairs," he said, pleased to have stated the obvious.

"Does it say four or five when we get to the fifth floor?"

"It says five," he replied, giving Toon an askance look. "Of course."

This reminded Guise of an incident on his first visit to Ireland, albeit the north. Between floors, and breaks to catch his breath, he recounted it to the others.

"It was the days of the Troubles," he said, "and so when the taxi dropped me off at the hotel I wasn't surprised to see a sign by the reinforced front door stating 'Door Locked for security. Please press bell to speak to Reception.' I pressed the bell and heard an Irish voice: 'Who's that?' it said. 'I'm a guest,' I replied. 'Oh, come in, guest.' And the door swung open. After checking in, I was handed a key. 'You're in Room 256,' said the receptionist. 'But this key says 132,' I pointed out. 'Yes, he replied,' they all say 132. Security!'

"Whoever was in Room 132," said Hayes, "was in for a busy night!"

*

On this, the boys' last evening in Ireland, it's worth reflecting on one important question: how do Irish pubs differ from English pubs? Let us name the ways.

- For a start they're usually neither 'pubs' nor 'inns', but 'bars'.
- Rather than being named after an improbably coloured animal (Red Lion, Blue Monkey) or neatly severed human appendages (Saracen's Head, King's Arms – boom boom!), they're often named after the bar's owner, present or past, such as three of those visited by the boys that night in Tralee: Quinlan's, Paddy Mac's and Sean Og's. Devilishly simple.
- Most often, as used to be the case in England, you can't see inside from out: no doubt a ruse to protect the anonymity of the drinkers – until the moment they fall out onto the pavement and into the beefy arms of their beloveds, of course.
- As we've seen, whole areas of the place may be deserted, for theoretical use by theoretically light drinkers, viz. women and priests. (Pull the other one...)
- The selection of drinks on offer is usually slim and awful. Quinlan's, for example, was yet another that offered just cold Guinness or cold lager. Rather like an ironmonger's stocked entirely with half-inch screws and door-knobs.
- Finally – and this is where Ireland scores a potential winner – not

only are the locals prepared to talk to new customers and keen to answer every enquiry, they often submit each newcomer to an in-depth personal interrogation: 'You're after looking down in the mouth: what's up?', 'Where are your wives, now, and who are they with?' or 'You've no children yourself? Why's that then?'

*

As McDonald and Toon were still arguing over bathroom time at the digs, Hayes and Guise arrived as a two-man vanguard in Quinlan's. It was as though the twenty-first century had been left outside. The creaky door opened onto an entirely deserted bar smelling of polished wood and old coal fires. The subdued muttering from a back room drew them through a set of ancient swing doors into another bar. As they entered, the muttering swiftly stopped. Two men hunched over a small table stared at the new arrivals, one man at the bar tottered backwards before steadying himself on a bar stool and a second simply glared, his pint frozen between bar and mouth. The only woman in the room was the probable landlady, a short woman of ample girth, motherly dress and suspicious gaze.

After Guise had broken the silence with their order, and with it vocal confirmation of their nationality, the regulars returned half their attention to their business. The unsteady barfly made his business the sporting credentials of these Englishmen and once they'd recalled Liverpool's heroics of the previous night, everyone seemed to relax a little.

"Here's a man with a small head and a big hat," said one of the seated duo as Toon came in.

"And here's another with a big head and a big hat," said his mate as McDonald followed him.

Whether they were practising their descriptions in case subsequently interviewed as witnesses by the *Garda* was unclear. But anyway, by the time the boys left, all seemed relaxed and they'd even gleaned some more recommendations for the bar crawl.

After Paddy Mac's (more pub than bar) and four hefty plates of fish and chips at another Quinlan's, they found themselves in a very full and very noisy venue: *An Chearnóg* (The Square). The noise was threefold: the usual chatter of the customers, a duo of guitar and Irish whistle playing away in the corner plus, bizarrely and quite annoyingly, a raucous television fixed immediately above the musicians and half-drowning their excellent folk music with a hideous cacophony. Oddest of all was that no one, least of all the two musicians, paid any heed whatsoever to this ear-punishing clash. Meanwhile, seated in another corner, the boys were straining to focus not only on their pints but on an intense discourse being delivered, free, *gratis* and for their ears only by a short man in a red coat.

Back at the bar, in his usual, recklessly gregarious way, McDonald had broached the controversial subjects of the Easter Rising, the subsequent executions and the long-standing political tension between the Irish and the British, stressing that, as far as he was concerned, some questions remained unanswered. Perhaps he simply wanted to add the noise of a quick bar fight to the general mayhem. Whatever, the result was that, in their praiseworthy mission to complete the education of any visitor in the history of the Irish Republic, the locals had despatched the red-coated gentleman to the Englishmen's table.

"Someone here wants executing?" he started, somewhat ominously. "I mean someone here wants to know about the 1916 executions?"

His Highness admitted it was him.

"Well," he explained, "Patrick Pearse was of course the first. Facing the firing squad the same day was Thomas MacDonagh of the Irish Volunteers, as was Tom Clarke of the Republican Brotherhood..."

"What were all these organisations?" asked McDonald, before regretting the question for the next thirty minutes.

It turned out that Red Coat was an historian of some repute and factions within the Republican movement were his speciality. Once more the boys had voluntarily opened themselves up to the attention of someone with several On switches but no Off switch. From the missing submarine, via the Irish Citizen Army and confusions in Galway to the trial of Roger Casement... the boys got exactly what they'd asked for: a blow-by-blow account of 1916. After a while, they began to wonder if the story of Ireland's struggle for freedom would continue till the end of 2016. Eventually though their glasses were empty, Red Coat's order at the bar was full and all left somewhat older and possibly wiser.

Travelling in Ireland, Lesson 32: Never ask an Irishman to tell you all he knows about anything.

*

Last call was a venue equally noisy but packed with patrons at least a generation younger. Since some of these were female, Hayes' interest was predictably aroused, but on this occasion McDonald got in first and tried his luck (or queered Hayes' pitch, depending on who you believe) with two thirty-somethings sitting some way back from the bar. After a brief and productive exchange of views (or a brush-off, depending on who you believe), he withdrew, supped up and left for an early bath. With Hayes still on the scent though, Guise and Toon stayed to watch the entertainment. And within five minutes he'd duly obliged.

The live band having moved on to an Irish jig, the Councillor first practised a few nifty moves on the spot before jigging his way towards two *twenty*-somethings who'd settled at a table not far away. After getting what looked from a distance like a look of cold steel, he neatly swayed on his heel and jigged back to the boys' table.

"Were they warming to you?" asked Guise.

"Well, they're just not ready for me yet," explained Hayes. "That's all."

Before he could lower his target age group by yet another decade, the Captain and the Skipper decided to escort the Jigging Councillor safely from the premises. And for once things were just as they should be on a boys' outing: no one could remember what time this particular evening ended.

Peggy of Minnesota tries to decide who's the 'ass' in 'Three Men and an Ass'.

They seek him here...

They seek him there...

They seek Fungie the Dolphin everywhere. (He's behind you...)

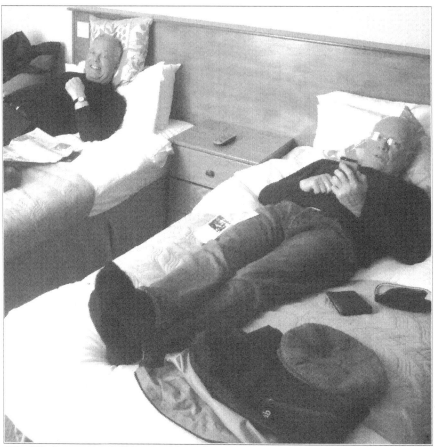

His Highness and Skipper Toon hard at work discussing bathroom rights in Tralee.

Running on

Empty

Saturday, Tralee to Quorn.

It was an uncharacteristically low-key foursome that was served breakfast by the sprightly East European waitress at the Tralee Townhouse. Hayes was reflective, having woken up at three o'clock still wearing his specs; Guise had his thickish head in a railway timetable; McDonald seemed exhausted; and Toon was – how can we put this delicately? – hung over.

"It can't have been the beer," he reasoned (beer being a recuperative medicine in ToonWorld). "Must have been the chips." Of course.

Slightly revived by the half-hour walk to the station, they assembled on the platform.

"Where are the tracks?" asked McDonald. It was a fair question, there being nothing but gravel beyond the platform edge.

"Probably under that train over there," suggested Guise. And indeed over to the east, some way out of the train shed, they could just see the smart grey-and-green livery of faithful old Iron Rod.

Flopping into their seats, the boys soon quietened their own ramblings to eavesdrop on the conversation of two youths behind them. 'Fecks' and 'f*cks' seem to be liberally used by the Irish, of both sexes and all ages. The youth dominating this conversation favoured the full 'f*ck', but for those of a nervous disposition (the current writer, for example) they're replaced here with 'fecks'. His conversational style could be termed 'rapid-fire'.

"D'yagetone'o'thosefeckinTVlicences,d'ya?" he asked his friend.

"Orr, now I think I might have," he replied, at normal pace.

"Igotoneferafiftypercentfeckindiscountandnowthefeckerstellmeit'safeck-infake!"

"A fake? A real fake?"

"Whatyerfeckinsayinyerfeckinidiot? A*real*fake?! Afeckinfake'safeckin-fakeferfeck'ssake. NowIgottapaythefeckersahundredanfiftyfeckineurosfer-arealoneplusafiftyfeckineurosfeckinfine! Feckthefeckin'feckers!"

Sitting with the pair was a young boy of about three, presumably the son of the normal-paced youth, for just before the train departed they got out, leaving Rapid Fire to feckin' fume on his feckin' own. With such conversation as a backdrop, you might imagine the child's demands on being returned to his mother...

"Where'smefeckinfoodyerfeckinmam?"

"You two've been hanging around with Dermot again, haven't you?"

Back on the train, another lad of about twenty-one engaged the Councillor in a more genial conversation. He was keen to recommend a certain hotel in Killarney where he happened to be the new chef. Hayes explained that they were only changing trains in Killarney, but listened politely to the boy's lengthy assessment of the catering course he'd just completed.

"How long's the training?" asked Hayes in his usual strong accent.

The lad looked a little hurt.

"It's forty minutes to Killarney," he said, before slumping back into his seat.

These rude Londoners, they're not interested in us at all!

*

After changing at Mallow, Captain Careful decided it was time for a financial summit. Apart from the drinks kitty, he'd kept a note of who'd paid which bill for meals and accommodation, done a few sums and come up with three transactions that would settle the whole thing: McDonald and Hayes would pay him two separate amounts and in addition Hayes would pay Toon another amount. Hayes and Toon were relaxed with this and Hayes happily paid up. Throughout the Captain's discourse, however, McDonald had been silent. He now expressed his concern.

"Not so fast, Guisey. We've all paid something on behalf of all three, so we should all owe everyone else something."

"I've gone beyond that," explained Guise.

"What do you mean?"

"I've replaced six transactions with three that come to the same thing."

McDonald was still perplexed. This is a man who's masterminded hundreds of thousands of pounds' worth of payments, loans and debts on enough dwellings to house half of Christendom. But after six days with these three, his little grey cells were running on empty.

"Prove it!" he challenged.

So, one by one, Guise addressed the others, specifying how much they'd paid, how much they should have paid and therefore what the difference was.

McDonald was almost convinced, but demanded one last piece of evidence.

"Now you," he said. "Do it to yourself."

With the patience of a Celtic saint, Guise proceeded to speak loudly and deliberately to himself.

"OK, Guise. You paid £422.20, right? Right. You should have paid £187.60, right? Right. Therefore you are owed £234.60, right? Right. And you're going to receive £187.60 plus £47, which equals...? £234.60, sir. The two figures are therefore the same, right? Right. Thank you. Pleasure."

A small ripple of applause came from the seat behind.

"All right," conceded His Highness. "I give in."

*

To the sound of the train announcer thanking them one more time 'for travelling neither here nor there', they descended once more onto the platform of Dublin Heuston. With an hour to kill, there was just enough time to skip over the road to Collins Barracks.

Known under the British as the Royal Barracks before being handed over to the Irish Free State in 1922, this sprawling complex by the banks of the Liffey was built in 1702 and was claimed to be the oldest continuously occupied barracks in the world before it was finally taken over by the National Museum of Ireland in 1997. As part of the commemoration of the Easter Rising, it was hosting an exhibition entitled 'Proclaiming the Republic' and it was to this that the boys were headed.

Less skipping than limping some way behind the others was Captain Careful. While McDonald was mentally exhausted, Guise seemed to be physically struggling and spent forty of the forty-five minutes at the Barracks slumped in a chair outside the cafe wondering how many details of revolutionary zeal any man may actually need in his lifetime. Duly revived, however, he re-joined the others on the trek back to the station where it was decided they could miss one bus for the sake of a pint at the Galway Hooker. Time to check they'd all still got their return tickets to the airport.

Guise: "Yes."

Toon: "Yes."

Hayes: "No."

McDonald: "No."

While the Councillor seemed less than surprised that he'd mislaid his, McDonald unpacked his entire documentary belongings onto the table. In vain. Even boarding the coach, he was still searching his pockets but in the end had to admit defeat and pay up... before slumping into a seat away from the others and glaring at the football results on his smartphone. By O'Connell Street he'd cheered up.

"Ha! Villa have been relegated. Not before time."

Toon meanwhile had recovered from his hangover. As they cruised along the airport travelator, he seemed particularly excited that they'd be arriving at the departure gate only just in time.

"My wife would be on the floor with stress by now," he revealed.

The only one of the four who was breezing through the last day as bright-eyed and bushy-tailed as he'd been on the first was Councillor Hayes.

"Hey, chaps," he said, moving towards the other three as they queued to board the aircraft. "I know we've all grown beards – well, Guisey's grown his longer than usual – but I've just bought some new after-shave. Tell me what you think." He edged closer.

"*I'm* not going to smell you," stated Toon.

"Get away, you fool!" said McDonald.

"Ugh!" said Guise.

"Please yourselves," said Hayes and proceeded to wander nonchalantly as near to a well-dressed lady passenger as he dare...

*

Following an uneventful flight (unless you count Toon's suggestion that, as they were flying over North Wales, they might catch a glimpse of Everest – an atlas of ToonWorld will be published shortly), the boys landed at East Midlands at nine o'clock. Just enough time for a pint in Loughborough. After five days suffering the cold ball-bearing treatment from Guinness, the soft, smooth draughts of Vixen, a local ale from Charnwood Brewery, went down like nectar from heaven.

Back in Quorn and – what do you know? – the White Hart was still open. Well, why not? So it was back to the map table where the journey had begun for one last pint.

"Well," admitted Guise, "young Dermot was right. The Dingle Peninsula was fabulous."

"Yep, fair do's," added McDonald. "Couldn't have found anywhere better."

"And we should thank the Councillor," suggested Toon, "for coming up with the idea..."

But the Councillor's attentions seemed to be focused on the bar.

"You know, I think that gel at the end's on 'er own. I wonder if she wants to hear about a week's adventure in Ireland..."

Tralee: the railway station with no railway.

*Hats of heroes (or rebels), some with ominous holes, at the
'Proclaiming a Republic: The 1916 Rising' exhibition, Collins
Barracks, Dublin.*

Post-Amble

Six days later, the boys joined their other chums and other halves at their regular Friday-night venue, not the White Hart but the Royal Oak (or Antonio's Bar, as it would be called in Ireland). As a treat for the other clientele, they'd come in their Murphy's tee-shirts and equipped with swanee whistles. Unfortunately they hadn't practised anything and so the performance lasted about three seconds before the wincing majority won. The thought was there though.

"Right, chaps," said McDonald, now back to his 'amazing, mesmerising' self. "Where were we this time last week?"

As Guise and Hayes cast their minds back to the west of Ireland, Toon jumped in with his best guess:

"We were here," he said.

Safely back at the Royal Oak, Quorn. All seem to be fingering the swanee whistles in their pockets, but who didn't read the memo about cloth caps and beer? (Photo: V. McDonald)

For more copies of this book,
go to
www.amazon.co.uk
or
www.lulu.com
or
contact the author at richard_guise@yahoo.com

Other Books by Richard Guise

Neddytown: A History of Draycott and Church Wilne (2001; Lulu, 2014)

Lead Us Not Into Trent Station (2003; Lulu, 2014)

Limerick Gazetteer of Europe (2004)

From the Mull to the Cape (Summersdale, 2008)

Over the Hill and Round the Bend (Summersdale, 2009)

Two Wheels Over Catalonia (Summersdale, 2011)

A Wiggly Way Through England (Lulu, 2013)

Nothing Between Here and The Urals? (2014)

Dictionary of Irritants (2014 and 2015)

The Extraordinary Life of Harry Quiningborough (expected 2016)

Writing as George Quin:

Murder in Minsk (2015)

Those in stock are available through bookshops, via www.amazon.co.uk or via www.lulu.com.

17946350R00071

Printed in Great Britain
by Amazon